1001 IDEAS FOR OUTDOOR SPACES

1001 IDEAS FOR OUTDOOR SPACES

THE ULTIMATE SOURCEBOOK:
Decking, Paving, Designs, and Accessories

BRETT MARTIN

Creative Publishing
international

First published in North America in 2008 by
Creative Publishing International
400 First Avenue North
Suite 300
Minneapolis, MN 55401
800 328 3895
www.creativepub.com

Creative Publishing
international

A Marshall Edition
Conceived, edited, and designed by
Marshall Editions
The Old Brewery
6 Blundell Street
London N7 9BH
U.K.
www.marshalleditions.com

ISBN-10: 1–58923–386–7
ISBN-13: 978–1–58923–386–7

A catalog record for this book is available from the
Library of Congress

Current printing (last digit)
10 9 8 7 6 5 4 3

Originated in Hong Kong by Modern Age
Printed and bound in Singapore

Publisher: Richard Green
Commissioning editor: Claudia Martin
Art director: Ivo Marloh
Illustrators: Ana Maria Diaz and Mark Franklin
Design and editorial: Seagull Design
Project editor: Amy Head
Indexer: Lisa Footit
Production: Nikki Ingram

Contents

Introduction

Creating outdoor living space is more popular than ever, and for good reason. We all want a place to relax outside with family and friends, soak up the sun, and experience nature. Decks and patios provide all that, and more. They transform your yard into a functional, attractive space that lets you feel just as much at home outside as you do inside.

Decks and patios blur the lines between the indoors and the outdoors. Decks offer a place to sit down and socialize outside, yet they still serve as part of the house. Patios located in front of entry doors welcome guests and visitors by softening the transition from the outside space into the house. Decks and patios can be located in the yard, offering a secluded area away from the house.

By extending your living area, decks and patios make your home feel more spacious. They are essentially outdoor rooms and can offer similar amenities to other rooms in the house. You might cook on a full-service kitchen complete with dining area, soak in a hot tub, or unwind and enjoy a nap in the sun.

A deck or patio can be added to any home, and existing decks and patios can be upgraded or accessorized to meet your needs. They can complement your house and yard, or they can become the focal point of your outdoor space. There's almost no limit to what you can do or add to decks and patios.

This book shows the range of possibilities for beautiful decks and patios for any home, yard, or landscape. It provides comprehensive ideas for planning, beautifying, and enhancing your outdoor space. The following chapters cover everything from expansive dream decks and patios to practical projects that can make your outdoor space more functional. Whether you have a compact lot, a roof-top terrace, or wide open space, you'll find proven ideas that will meet your needs.

Features such as barbecue areas, attractive arbors, and lighting are described and illustrated in detail, as are ideas for adding pathways, plant life, and overhead shade structures. Expert advice for choosing patterns, materials, and colors is also offered.

We live in a staggering range of climates, have diverse lifestyles, and differ in our tastes. Budget considerations vary from household to household. In the end, as the indoor areas of your home are, the outdoor space you live in will be unique to you.

Opposite: Mixing wood and concrete gives this multi-level deck an inspiring blend of colors and textures. Cable railings have a modern look that fits the contemporary theme.

Below: A variety of materials, in warm, contrasting colors, surround this circular pool.

Evaluating Your Home

The shape and slope of your yard greatly influence your options for building or expanding a deck or patio. Yards are purposely designed to slope gradually away from the house. This directs rainwater away from the foundation so it doesn't leak into the basement. Patios should also have a very subtle slope of 1 inch for every 8 to 10 feet of surface.

Almost any deck and patio design will work with level terrain, but rolling areas can present a challenge, especially for patios. Severe slopes require grading so the patio surface will be flat. Installing retaining walls along the patio or pathway or splitting the patio into tiers are two popular ways to handle sloping landscapes.

Decks are less affected by slopes than patios since they can be built over any terrain, but the yard's contour will help determine the best type

of deck for your landscape. A platform deck built at ground level works well for flat yards, while raised decks conquer slopes that would otherwise be unusable. Multi-level decks are often built at different heights to follow sloping yards that might otherwise be difficult to use.

Incorporate the existing features of your yard into your design. Trees and flower gardens make excellent borders, so consider expanding the deck or patio to adjoin the foliage. You can even build around trees so they rise up through the decking or patio surface. If an existing fence or wall closes off an area of your property, it's a great place for a private retreat.

Swimming pools usually have an attached area for relaxation, which can be expanded to include a more formal patio or deck, perhaps with an

① Several shapes come together to create the unique profile of this inside corner deck. The curved left side leads to square stairs, while hard angles define the right side.

② Lights are placed across the deck and gazebo to make this outdoor space usable day and night. The lights illuminate the space without being too bright.

③ The extremes of fire and water, combined with wood and stone, mix several colors and textures in this compact patio.

outdoor kitchen and dining areas. A pathway or walkway is perfect for connecting the pool to a deck, patio, or even a gazebo.

Your deck or patio should complement your house, landscape, and features such as fences and gardens. Using the same colors is an easy way to strike a balance, like painting or staining a wooden deck to match the house's trim color. Something as simple as setting the same plants on your deck and patio that already grow in your yard will also create coherence. And while you want to strive for harmony between decks and patios and their surroundings, it's also good to let them have their own identities. Adding a curve along the front of the deck or placing an inviting mosaic in the patio surface adds character and appeal without breaking the bank.

Planning Your Deck and Patio

Decks and patios are all about the views. You want to be able to sit outside and enjoy picturesque scenes of oceans, lakes, mountains, hillsides, woods, or gardens. All you have to do is find the place in your yard that offers the best view, then orient the deck or patio to capture that setting.

Walk around your house and yard to determine the location that offers the optimal view. Even if you've already picked a spot for the deck or patio, it's still worth taking a walk around to make sure you've selected the best place. You may decide to expand the deck or patio to attain a better view; lowering a section of the deck so you can see a water garden at ground level, for instance, or wrapping the back-yard patio around the side of the house to experience views from two directions.

Once you find the site that offers the best view, make sure it won't interfere with views from the house. You don't want a raised deck with a trellis to block the view from the living room. Also consider how the placement of the deck or patio will affect your home's curb appeal. Back-yard structures shouldn't affect the way the home looks from the street, but anything along the front or the sides will.

Don't forget the accessories. Include electrical and plumbing features in your plan. Adding electrical lights or electronically powered water features to a deck or patio requires running electrical cable out to the yard. Installing a hot tub requires plumbing. Likewise, plan for accessories such as trellises, built-in furniture, and fire pits. It's better to integrate them into the deck or patio as they're being built than to add them later.

① This elevated deck with decorative metal railings offers a spectacular view of a lake. The deck is high enough to allow people to see over the tops of nearby trees.

② Perfectly located to capture the ideal view, this deck has plenty of space for taking it all in while sitting outside.

③ Surrounded by greenery, this raised deck overlooks the entire yard, yet enjoys the shade of nearby trees.

④ A carefully planned design means the lake in the background here seems like a natural extension of the raised pool in the patio.

Finding the Space You Need

Deck and patio projects are limited in scope by three factors: local building codes, your budget, and available space. You're required to adhere to building codes, and your budget depends on circumstance, but with some careful planning and ingenuity, you can nearly always find space for a deck or patio.

Look beyond the immediate area around the house and consider space across the entire yard. For small lots, build a raised deck so you can still use the yard beneath it—or turn the space underneath into a patio. You can also steal part of a small lawn to use for a paved patio, garden, or water feature. If space is exceptionally tight, add a narrow deck along the back of the house or turn the driveway into a patio.

Building a patio in the front yard, then winding an attached pathway or walkway through to the back yard can make a confined area seem larger. Incorporating an elaborate design in the deck or patio, such as an interesting pattern in the decking or paving, can

An entry patio leads to the front door on this small lot, while a ground-level deck extends across the back yard. A privacy fence, trees, and shrubs enclose the yard, secluding it from neighbors.

also give the illusion of larger space. For really tiny areas, think vertically. Anything that draws the eye upward, like an arbor or tall skinny trees, will make the area appear larger.

Large yards give you more options, but the deck and patio still need to follow a coordinated plan. Open spaces give you the freedom to add more features—like a pond, trellis, or raised garden bed—but it's important to keep them in harmony to avoid a hodgepodge of contrasting or competing features across the yard. Repeating colors, materials, or accents is one way to tie all of the elements together.

Make a drawing of your house and yard on paper. Use graph paper to help keep everything to scale. Be sure to include everything that's in your yard, such as trees, the driveway, fences, and sheds. This drawing lets you see opportunities for a deck and patio that you otherwise may have missed. It also helps you find space hidden in inside corners or under trees that could make an ideal location for a cozy patio.

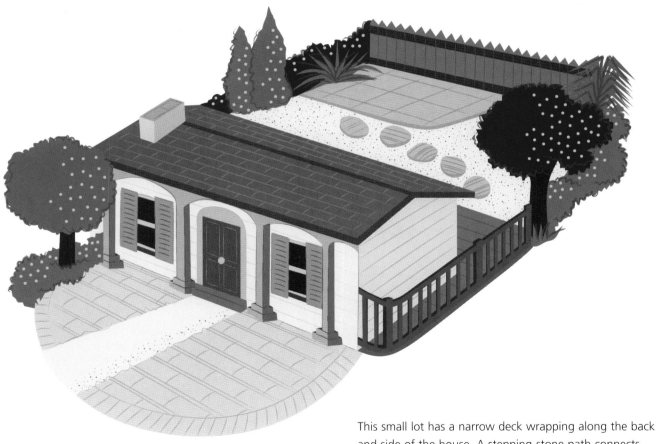

This small lot has a narrow deck wrapping along the back and side of the house. A stepping-stone path connects the deck to the detached patio in the back corner.

An outdoor space begins right outside your door, and large lots like these give you ample space to include everything you want for an enjoyable, functional outdoor room. The decks and patios shown here use the lot space to its fullest potential. All of the components and accessories integrate well together in the allotted space.

A deck spans the back of this house, with a table and chairs providing a place to sit. The deck gives way to a spacious patio and water garden, complete with spraying fountain. Placing a fence along the border ensures privacy. Trees and potted plants add greenery and flowers.

A multi-level deck steps down in tiers to a pool-surround patio here. The patio provides plenty of space for sunbathing around the swimming pool. A masonry retaining wall encircling the outdoor space supports foliage and clearly defines the patio's boundaries.

Designing Spaces

Regardless of the shape and size you choose for your deck or patio, you can design it specifically to be located out in the open, hidden from view, or somewhere in between.

One option is to place the deck or patio away from the house and any other structures (a shed or playhouse, for example) to maximize the wide open space. Keep furnishings and accessories to a bare minimum to ensure that obstacles won't interrupt a magnificent view.

At the other end of the spectrum is carving out a niche in a secluded area, surrounded by woods, tall plants, a fence, or a vine-covered arbor. This offers a private retreat where you can surround yourself with nature and enjoy the outdoors without being seen. If you don't have existing cover for privacy, use a fence or privacy screen to provide a retreat.

① Four pathways lead to this circular stone patio, which resembles an ancient sundial. The shrubs around the patio accentuate its shape.

② This figure-eight-shaped pool with tiled surround is well away from trees and overhead structures, so it receives direct sunlight.

③ Located away from the house, this wooden patio surface offers a solitary retreat in the corner of the yard.

④ This getaway deck takes full advantage of the lake setting and is slightly elevated to provide a better view.

Take advantage of borders surrounding the deck or patio. As well as providing decorative interest, shrubs, a tree line, a wall, or a fence can block out things you don't want to see, such as a neighbor's house or a busy street. They can also reduce noise.

Make detailed drawings of your house and yard, including existing features that will influence your design—a lawn or a tree you want to retain, for example—and then fill in your deck, patio, and anything else you'll be adding, such as flower gardens, a play area, or a water garden. Make as many copies as you need and play around with different ideas until you find your perfect design. This process will help you to make the most of all the options open to you.

①

Sun and Shade

Ideally, you can locate your deck or patio to provide the right degree of sun or shade. Keep in mind that the amount of sunlight reaching your outdoor space will change throughout the day. Take pictures of the proposed deck or patio site at different times during the day to see how much sun it gets. Areas that receive sun in the morning may be shaded by mid-afternoon, so find out how much direct sunlight your proposed deck or patio area gets at the times you're most likely to use it.

In general, decks and patios that face the north receive little sun, while those facing the south are in the sun all day long. East-facing structures receive sunlight in the morning, which is great if you want to sit in the sun and drink your morning coffee. Those facing the west tend to get the hot mid- to late-afternoon sun and sometimes a glare as the sun sets.

You can usually control, at least to some degree, the amount of sun or shade the deck or patio gets. If you want more sun, remove or trim back any trees, or extend the deck or patio into an area that receives direct sunlight.

Conversely, if you want more shade, plant more trees. Maples are a good choice because they grow fast and have large leaves, but any tree will work. Planting them southwest of the deck or patio will offer the most shade protection during the hottest part of the day—the afternoon. Trees also provide landscaping, which is another benefit. The drawback is that they won't provide immediate relief. They'll take at least five years to grow large enough to block the sun, so you'll need to make them part of your long-term plans.

For short-term relief, install a shade structure. A simple awning attached to the house can extend over part of the deck or patio for partial shade. Some are retractable, allowing you to control how much sunlight reaches you. Funky, colorful sun sails are especially versatile. Larger awnings and overhead canopies can cover the entire deck or patio, and can be opened and closed as desired.

① The awning above this deck provides shade during the hot afternoon, but in the morning the sun shines directly onto the patio, providing warmth early in the day.

② This triangular roof construction provides shade and shelter for part of the patio. Lush, flowering climbers soften the formal effect of the pillars.

③ Closely spaced slats on this overhead structure cut the amount of sunlight that reaches the patio. The other half of the patio receives full sun.

④ This terra-cotta-tiled patio roof, built over solid wooden beams, doesn't only provide shade, it also creates a permanent outdoor room.

⑤ This curving patio cuts a path between the trees, which keep the surface shaded and reduce exposure to wind.

Creating Outdoor Rooms

Once you decide on the location of your deck and patio, you can start creating your outdoor room. Decide what you want to include on the structure, such as a cooking area, dining area, or whirlpool. Also decide where such features will go. Cooking areas are usually located away from the house so the smoke can easily dissipate and won't discolor the siding. Whirlpools are usually closer to the house for privacy.

Function is just as important as looks, so plan the design around the activities that will take place on the deck or patio. If the primary function will be entertaining, have plenty of space where guests can gather without being separated by barriers. If it's relaxing, have comfortable places to sit down. If it's enjoying nature, bring plants onto the deck or patio.

Think of the space as an actual room. Your decking or paving serves as the floor. You can add retaining walls, fences, or screens as the walls, and an arbor or trellis for the ceiling. Plan for either built-in or portable furniture so you'll have places to sit, and lights so you can use the area at night. Decide where you want to place any stairs and where people will enter and exit.

Like other rooms, decks and patios should look inviting. Attractive colors, vibrant foliage, and striking views should draw guests outside. Comfort will convince them to stay.

① Evenly spaced lights keep this patio well lit. During the day, a portable awning provides shade.

② This long, narrow water feature extends into the patio, offering the peaceful sound of a controlled waterfall.

③ Designed with entertainment in mind, this patio has an outdoor table that comfortably seats up to eight people.

④ This deck is broken up into several sections, or "rooms," each for a different function, such as soaking in the hot tub or cooking on the grill.

Designing Decks

Building a well-planned and integrated deck is an inexpensive way to expand your living space while adding beauty and value to your home. When planning your deck, a vital consideration is just how you would like to use it—whether for relaxing, socializing, or dining. Take into account the views you would like to capture or avoid, the space available, and the style of your home and garden. Not least to consider are practicalities such as budget, as well as options for heating and shelter.

Opposite: This raised, square deck is connected to a rectangular platform deck by stairs. The lower deck is furnished for dining.

Below: A wavy front edge adds visual interest to this deck, especially since the railing follows the same curves.

As an extension of the house, the deck is like another room in the home, which means you can design or modify it to serve your needs. Plan a second story or elevated deck to make the most of picturesque views, or wrap the deck around the side and back of the house to take in views from several directions. A multi-level deck can connect each level of the house and make the most of sloping yards, while adding a low-profile platform deck will increase the living space around a ground-level entry.

Decks can work with any landscape. If your yard is sloped and doesn't get a lot of use, a deck will utilize the space, providing a comfortable outdoor haven. If you have an L- or U-shaped house and cannot capitalize on the inside corner space, a deck can solve the problem by bridging the adjacent walls. Even if you are lacking space, a long, narrow deck running along the back of the house will make the area more appealing. Unlike a front porch that is exposed to street traffic, the deck can afford a greater degree of privacy. Trellises, arbors, and screens can be cleverly employed to allow any necessary degree of seclusion.

When planning your design, you don't have to settle for a flat, box-shaped deck. There is a seemingly endless number of shapes and styles to choose from, including circular decks, angular decks, multi-level decks, and decks that span the entire length of the house. And there is always the opportunity to make functional features double as design elements, specifically stairs and railings.

Square Decks

A square deck is easy to design and build, which makes it a good choice for tight budgets or do-it-yourselfers with minimal construction experience. These decks are box-shaped, with a symmetrical profile that will fit the style of almost any house. Despite its basic shape, a square deck can be dressed up to look more enticing. Even a simple trellis or ornate railing adds an extra dimension. An interesting decking pattern is another easy way to add pizzazz.

① This compact deck provides seating right outside the back door. A vertical skirt makes the structure look taller and finishes the underside of the deck.

② Raised planters alongside the stairs welcome guests onto this perfectly square deck. There's plenty of room for a table-and-chair set and a barbecue grill.

③ The outer walls of this house screen the side and corner of the vinyl platform deck. A privacy fence, also finished with vinyl, blocks the view of the neighboring house, leaving the rest of the deck open.

④ Spanning the width of the house, this square deck has stairs that lead to a concrete patio below. The deck and patio combined fill the entire back yard.

⑤ Laying the decking in a diagonal pattern has provided a more interesting effect here.

⑥ Railings provide safety along the two sides of this deck that are slightly raised, while the area adjoining the patio is completely open.

Rectangular Decks

The long, often narrow shape of a rectangular deck works really well when you want a deck that runs across most or all of the back of the house. This classic shape is one of the most popular deck styles. A rectangular deck offers a lot of space without extending too far out into the yard. It also lends itself well to stairs placed at one end. Make the deck versatile by using one side for one purpose, like cooking, and the other side for something else, like reclining in a hammock.

① Running along the back of the house, this rectangular deck is long enough to contain two sets of stairs, a pergola, a built-in bench, and furniture.

② The deck next to this house is built in two levels. A built-in bench makes good use of the corner farthest from the house, and screens provide privacy.

③ Here is a deck furnished with plenty of seating, a dining table at one end, an informal table set at the other end, and reclining chairs in the middle.

④ This angled rectangular deck is divided into distinct areas for sunbathing, dining, and relaxing in the hot tub.

⑤ Brightly painted white railings reflect the trim on the house. Matching chairs are spread around, providing plenty of space for quiet relaxation or socializing.

⑥ Just raised above the level of the lawn and with no railing, this deck has an open feel. Flowerpots link the two areas and add a splash of color.

⑦ This narrow strip of decking is partially shaded by the roof overhang on the house.

Round and Curved Decks

Consider a round deck if you want a captivating design that's sure to garner attention. Adding a curve gives a deck a distinctive look, which is why these decks are popular. You can round off the corners to eliminate hard edges, or turn the entire outward-facing side of the deck into a generous curve. Curves will soften the straight lines of the house, offering a feeling of serenity. Be aware that a round deck is more challenging to build, which means it will cost more or require more expertise if you take the job on yourself.

① This entire deck is circular, including the railing along the left side. An inlay with a yin-yang design further emphasizes the round shape.

② Elongated stairs follow the gentle curve of this deck. Every other stair is painted a different color to draw attention to the round edge.

③ This raised deck curves toward the treetops, creating a leisure area in a space that would otherwise be unused.

④ A curve in this deck's upper section matches the lower deck's round shape. A gazebo shelters the entire circular section from the elements.

⑤ All three components of the outdoor space—the deck, patio, and swimming pool—follow the same curves.

⑥ Four tiers of rounded stairs lead to the lower section of this deck, which feeds into two levels on either side of the house.

④

⑤

⑥

Angular Decks

If you're looking for an easy way to avoid conventional square corners, go with an angled deck. The corners are usually angled at or close to forty-five degrees, making the deck visually interesting. Play around with different geometric shapes to find a design you like. Putting angles on all four corners of the deck will give it an intriguing octagonal shape, similar to a gazebo. Since incorporating angles is inexpensive, it's a great way to make the deck look attractive without spending a lot of money.

① Soft angles are used on both of the raised sections on this deck: the platform to the left and the hot tub area.

② Regularly spaced corners jut out at forty-five degree angles to the building, giving this ground-level deck an intriguing look.

③ This deck's highest level, with a hot tub, is placed at an angle to the rest of the structure. In this position, the hot tub remains unified with the rest of the deck.

④ Eight equally spaced sides give the lower deck here an attractive octagonal shape. The upper level is angled to match the two sides nearest the house.

⑤ The front of this deck and the single step leading up to it are built at a comfortable angle that softens the linear look of the house, deck wall, and pergola.

⑥ With the house walls set at forty-five degree angles to each other, it seems natural for the deck to follow the same shape.

⑦ A series of angles define this platform deck. Varying levels, a built-in bench, and planters add extra interest.

Wraparound Decks

A wraparound deck is a good option when you want views from multiple perspectives. The deck that wraps around two or more sides of the house also gives you the option of moving from the sun into the shade, or vice versa. Wraparound decks usually sit near ground level and span two or more entryways. Because these decks turn corners, it's easy to separate them into sections for different activities. Building the front with a gentle curve makes it look more inviting than a hard right angle that matches the corner of the house.

① This front porch deck wraps around the front entrance, adjoins the gazebo, and then continues around the side of the house.

② Adorned with potted plants, this narrow deck wraps around a sun room that houses a whirlpool. The deck serves as an extension of the conservatory.

③ Starting out at ground level, this deck runs along the front of the house, becoming a raised deck by the time it reaches the back. The brick foundations under the deck posts match the house bricks.

④ This deck starts at the back entrance to the house, extends out at the corner, and connects to the screened-in porch. The white rails, stair risers, and lattice match the house trim.

⑤ This narrow deck acts like a balcony, surrounding the house and connecting entrances.

①

Inside Corner Decks

An inside corner deck is the obvious choice
for L-shaped and U-shaped houses. The deck
is installed along adjacent sides of the house,
capitalizing on space that might otherwise be
underutilized. Having house walls on two sides
provides privacy and intimacy, making these
decks ideal for whirlpools and sunbathing. The
walls also provide partial protection from wind
and sun, making the deck more comfortable.
Inside corner decks almost always sit at
ground level, so they are easy to surround
with flowers, shrubs, or trees.

① Extending along the entire back of the house, this deck
follows the same L-shape as the house itself. Two sliding
patio doors provide indoor/outdoor access.

② A deck-and-patio combination transforms this inside
corner into useful outdoor living space.

③ Building a deck didn't require removing the tree in this
back yard. Instead, the deck fills the corner space and
makes way for the tree.

④ Instead of railings, a built-in bench marks the outside
edge of this deck and unifies the area.

Platform Decks

A platform deck works well for single-level homes and flat yards. It sits at or near ground level, which puts it in contact with the yard. This makes it easy to integrate landscaping, flowers, trees, and the patio into the deck area's overall design. A platform deck is typically the easiest deck to build. Since homeowner associations and local zoning restrictions don't usually require railings, there are no barriers between the deck and surrounding area, offering a truly open space.

① Custom railings, multiple levels, and a simple pergola give this deck a rustic theme.

② This eye-catching pattern defines the deck space and creates a focal point. It is accentuated by the way the stairs follow the circular shape. An eclectic mix of accessories, like the fireplace and the window set in stone, add appeal.

③ Wide stairs make a seamless transition from the deck to the yard. The benches double as railings, marking the border while also offering seating.

④ An integrated decking pattern ties the leaf-shaped sections together, giving this spacious deck a unified look.

Raised Decks

Building a raised deck is the perfect way to add outdoor space to a second-story room, such as a living room or bedroom. It has the additional benefits of making the most of sloping yards and affording the best views. Finishing the underside of the deck allows you to use the space below as a patio, while adding stairs provides access to the yard.

① Giving this home a large outdoor area, this deck is raised a full story off the ground. A long stairway with a landing follows the slope to the ground.

② This deck is raised high enough to meet the sliding door, allowing people to walk from the house onto a level outdoor living area.

③ Transparent railings are ideal for raised decks since they don't obstruct the views. The tree growing through this deck provides natural shade.

④ Stairs connect this raised deck to a concrete sidewalk and a patio. The deck provides shade for the seating area below.

⑤ This two-tiered deck is elevated enough to allow for a full patio underneath at ground level.

⑥ This deck is raised particularly high off the ground, so it didn't make sense to include stairs, which would have taken up too much space.

Island and Peninsula Decks

Separated from the house, an island deck offers flexibility, as it can be placed anywhere in the yard. Consider this option if you can't find a convenient place to connect the deck to the house, or if you want a freestanding deck in a location that captures the best view or setting, such as under tall shade trees.

For a deck that's close to the house but not physically attached, you can't go wrong with a peninsula deck. These are placed near the house for convenient access. They connect to the house via walkways or stairs, which are usually made with the same material as the decking.

① Connected to the house by stairs, this peninsula deck is surrounded by nature on all sides.

② This freestanding island deck with a pergola enjoys a pleasant setting just off the pathway on the lawn, bordered by flowers and trees.

③ This island deck is built over the patio to form a fitting place for sunbathing and relaxing beside the pool.

④ A multi-level pier leads to a peninsula deck near the water's edge. This deck has fixed shade structures and benches, encouraging people to sit down and relish the view.

⑤ An enclosed gazebo at the front of this deck lets people decide between being sheltered and being outdoors, surrounded by trees.

⑥ A boathouse roof makes a perfect place for a deck here. A path and stairs lead out to the deck from the house.

⑦ Raised to accommodate a pool that sits on top of the ground, this deck provides a solid surface for swimmers getting in and out of the water. Railings encircle the pool for safety.

Multi-level Decks

This deck type is ideal for connecting the various levels of a multi-level house or for following a sloping yard. Composed of two or more sections joined by stairs or walkways, a multi-level deck offers maximum versatility since you can use each level for a different purpose. Sections of deck that step down to follow the contour of the yard give these structures dramatic looks. You can also build a multi-level deck on a flat yard to add interest, even if only a couple of steps separate the sections.

① Designed for a golf enthusiast, this deck has an area carved out for driving, then steps down in sections to follow the slope of the ground until it ends up around the putting green.

② The upper deck here is used for grilling, while the bottom deck, made from a different wood species, is used for eating and entertaining.

③ Just a step and a section of railing separate these two platforms, but that's enough to give them each their own identity and add interest.

④ This multi-level deck looks especially dramatic when it's lit up at night. Lights illuminate the wide stairs leading to the patio, then light the way to the upper level.

⑤ Built-in benches, railings, and parallel decking boards—all of these tie the levels of this deck together.

⑥ Here, the lower deck section sits close to the ground without obtrusive railings. There are railings on the raised deck in the background.

⑦ Acting as an elaborate landing, the lower level of this deck has an inviting octagonal shape. The upper level also has interesting angles and the same decorative railings.

Decking Components

To end up with a deck that looks good and fulfills its function, all of the components need to work together and strike a balance with each other. The deck railings should match the stair railings, and the stairs should match the decking. To achieve this cohesive style, use the same or complementary materials and colors for the decking, railings, and stairs. This works for built-in accessories as well, such as pergolas and benches. Using the same materials for different elements makes the accessories look like natural parts of the deck.

① Using different railings separates the top deck and the left-hand side of the lower deck from the right-hand side of the lower deck.

② Leading from the deck to the yard, the stair treads here match the decking, while the wooden railings that run across the deck and down the stairs are left natural.

③ The same siding planks running beneath the deck and the stairs creates a consistent look. The railings also tie it all together.

④ Plastic balusters have been used in the stair railings here rather than the glass used for the railings on the upper deck, but the wood rails are the same throughout so the difference is less noticeable.

⑤ Most of the deck components here, including the decking, rails, steps, and benches, are made from the same wood species. The lattice wall breaks the railing pattern, but it still blends with the rest of the deck.

Decking

Decking boards are the most visible component of the deck. Planks may direct the eye to the stairs or the entrance to the house, and an intricate pattern might make the deck appear larger. Installing a border around the edge gives the deck a finished look. Composite decks can accommodate a colorful design, and this allows the decking to serve as a stunning focal point. Some patterns, like chevron (a V-shape), require more lumber and additional joist support, but it's worth the extra effort if you want an elaborate design.

① These stair treads are parallel to the stairs, but the decking itself is in a chevron pattern.

② Installing the decking parallel to the house emphasizes the length of this deck and leads the eye toward the stairs.

③ In angled decks like this one, aligning the decking with one side creates a pleasing design that's simple, yet effective.

④ Placing an inlaid design on decking gives the space instant appeal, and here breaks up the monotony of a box-shaped deck with repetitive straight lines.

⑤ Decking laid in different directions gives each level of this deck its own identity. A border defines the lower deck.

A pattern sets the aesthetic tone of a deck. Laying the boards straight gives the deck a calm, quiet feel; angled boards and patterns liven up the space by offering exciting designs; straight boards make small decks seem longer or wider; and patterns can stimulate an ordinary deck and transform a box-shaped structure into something more imaginative.

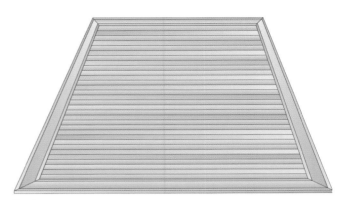

Border

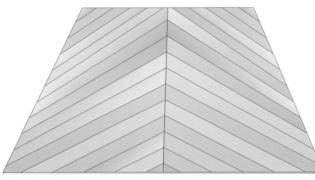

Double diagonal

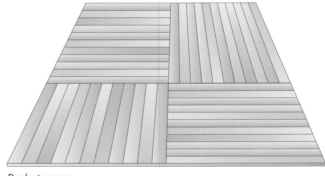

Basketweave

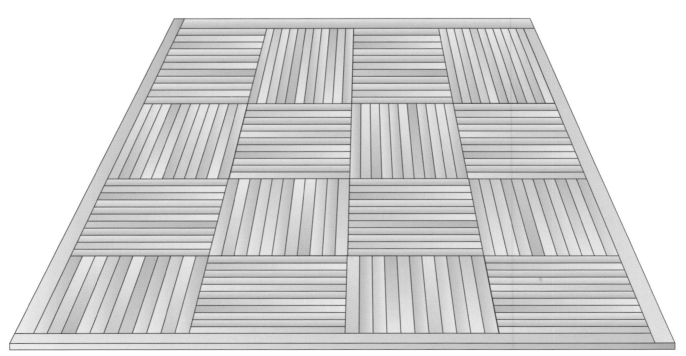

Parquet

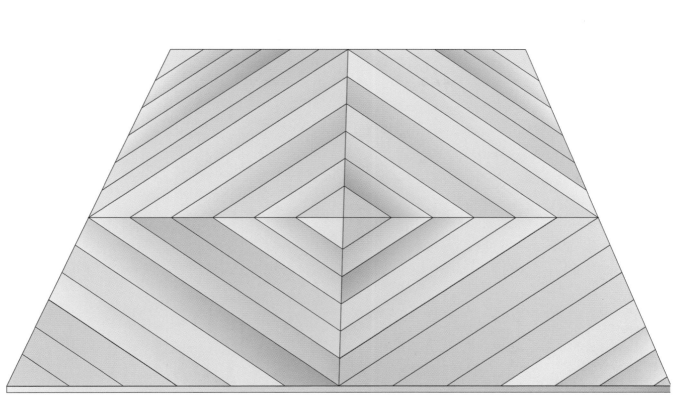

Diamond

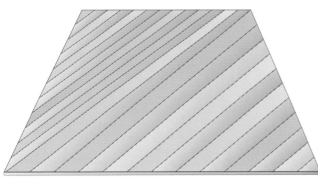

Diagonal

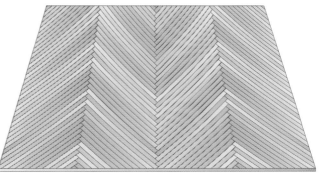

Herringbone

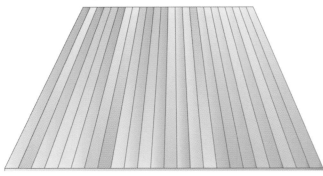

Perpendicular to house

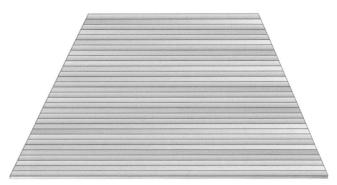

Parallel to house

Railings

Building codes are very particular about railing specifications, such as railing height, the amount of open space between the bottom of the railings and the deck, and the spacing between balusters. Besides serving as safety and protection, railings provide decoration. Vertical wood balusters are the most prevalent railings, but they're just one of many options. For an open view, consider acrylic or tempered glass.

① These metal sections are preassembled to form solid, decorative railings that are attached to low, broad columns for an upscale appearance.

② This vinyl railing surface is maintenance free and will never need painting.

③ The subtle curve created by these closely spaced metal rails offers a pleasing contrast to the straight lines created by the decking and posts.

④ Ornamental glass railings reflect the scenic landscape for a whimsical view of the surrounding trees.

⑤ The metal railing panel here interrupts the repetitive flow of the stock wood balusters to add a personal touch.

⑥ Custom panels like these are strictly for looks, not for safety. They should only be used on platform decks, which sit near ground level.

⑦ Completely transparent acrylic and tempered glass panels won't impede amazing views, such as this one. The modern railing system is a good match for the contemporary furniture and architecture.

⑧ Horizontal metal pipes allow for a better view of the wooded lot from this raised deck. The railings are durable, stylish, and maintenance free.

⑨ Slender balusters compose this common railing style. The classic design works with any type of deck.

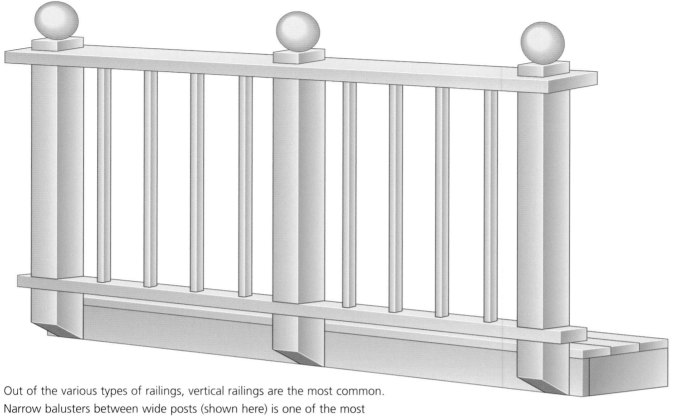

Out of the various types of railings, vertical railings are the most common.
Narrow balusters between wide posts (shown here) is one of the most
popular designs. The round finials over the posts add a sophisticated touch.

Horizontal railings aren't always made of wood. Quite often, they're made of cable or pipe, so it's
a great opportunity to incorporate steel or copper into the deck. This design is often used in the
decks of contemporary or ranch-style homes.

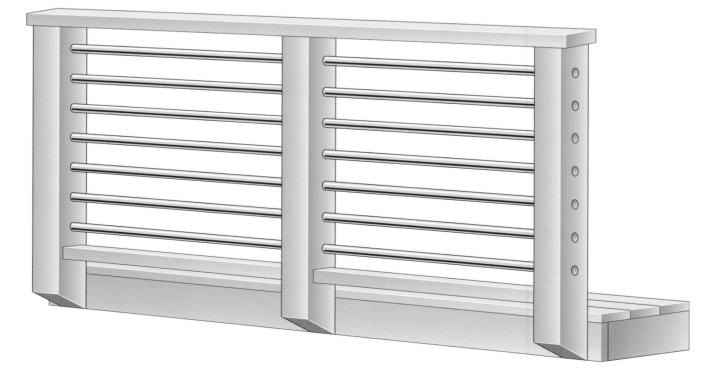

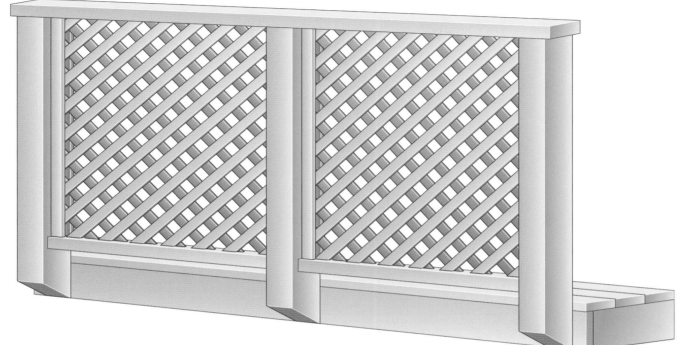

Lattice railings provide a good deal of privacy without fully enclosing the deck. The thin, crisscrossing panel design makes the railings more decorative than functional.

Wall-style railings enclose the deck completely, giving total privacy and restricting wind. These solid railings unify the deck with the house, making it seem more like an actual room.

Stairs

Stairs provide yard access and connect sections of multi-level decks. Consider breaking up long stairways into two sections by putting a landing in the middle. A landing also provides a platform for changing the direction of the stairs. Decide where you want the stairs when designing your deck so they don't end up protruding too far out into the yard. Also, choose the type of pad or landing you want at the bottom of the stairs. Popular options include stamped concrete and flagstone pavers.

① Winding along the side of the deck, then turning at a 90-degree angle to end under the deck, these stairs hardly protrude into the yard. They also make the attractive stairs a prominent part of the structure.

② Functional, elegant, and space-saving, this spiral steel staircase connects the first floor balcony with the concrete patio and the lawn beyond.

③ Painted the same warm yellow as the wall, these concrete stairs with terracotta slabs also tie in with the Spanish-style patio.

④ This short run of wide stairs ties the deck's upper section to the lower section.

⑤ Painting the stair treads and the riser boards different colors gives this expansive stairway an enticing look. It connects the deck to the pool area, then to the patio.

⑥ Omitting the riser boards between stair treads gives the stairs an open, airy feel. Since the stringers are now visible, they're painted to match the railings and contrast with the darker treads.

Deck Skirts

Deck skirts are installed between the decking and the ground. They wrap around the deck to provide a finished look and keep out animals. A skirt is typically used on decks that sit near the ground. Lattice is the most common skirt material, providing an inexpensive way to dress up the deck's exterior while still allowing free airflow. If you need access to the space under the deck (for storage, perhaps), simply design a gate or opening in the skirt.

① A vertical skirt makes this low-level deck appear higher off the ground and gives the surrounding space a cleaner look. The vertical lines contrast nicely with the horizontal lines of the facing boards.

② Here, a stone wall serves as the deck skirt, giving this structure a rugged appearance.

③ With its brown color, this skirt plays an inconspicuous role in the deck. The focus is on the brightly painted stairs and railing.

④ A simple strip of wood lattice is all that's needed to cover the opening between this deck and the ground. In turn, the skirt is hidden behind colorful foliage. The openings in the lattice allow air to circulate freely.

⑤ Horizontal boards accentuate this long deck, directing the eye to the stairs. The skirt design also makes the deck look very solid.

Privacy Walls

For privacy use tall, filled-in walls instead of railings. You don't need to install privacy walls all the way around the deck, just on the side or sides where you want to block the view, such as beside the hot tub or where you're in full view of the neighbors. Privacy fencing works well, as does lattice that's filled in with flowers or vines. If you use the same material as the house siding to enclose the entire structure, it makes the deck look like a part of the house.

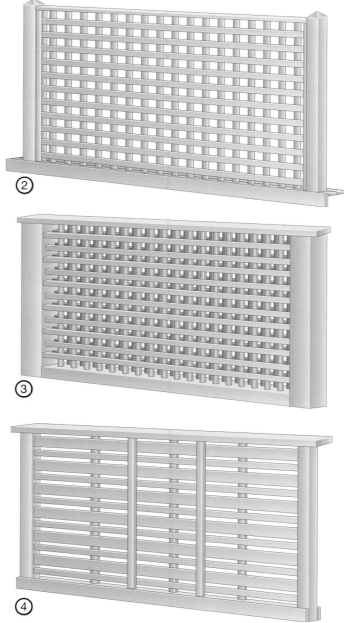

① This lattice privacy screen is placed over a typical vertical railing system for a two-tiered railing.

② A simple lattice panel placed between rail posts creates a basic, yet effective, privacy screen that doesn't completely obscure natural light.

③ Three layers of different-sized strips of wood interact to create a three-dimensional, complex screen that immediately captures attention.

④ Thin boards alternate with thick boards in this design, leaving narrow slats for airflow and sunlight. Regularly spaced vertical boards interrupt the horizontal lines.

⑤ A trellis is placed along only one side of the deck to provide privacy just where it is needed.

⑥ This structure has all the components of a typical room: the patio serves as the floor, the pergola serves as the roof, and the screens serve as the walls.

⑦ These clouded screens provide privacy for hot-tub users without blocking out the light. They're a great alternative to wood.

Planning Patios

A beautifully designed patio defines outdoor space and gives it character. From decorative patio surfaces to colorful gardens to tranquil water features, patios transform the yard into a functional living area that enhances and becomes a natural addition to the home. Detailed planning is essential, so decide how the space will be used, where the patio will be located, what spaces you want to connect, and what materials you want to use. You don't have to build everything at once. Once you have a plan, you can build in sections to suit your budget and allow time for the trees and foliage to fill in.

Opposite: Brick, stone, and concrete blend together nicely to create this multi-level contemporary patio. A retractable awning shades the table and chairs, while colorful foliage grows along the patio edges.

Below: This elevated patio offers a phenomenal city view in a comfortable outdoor setting.

Flexibility is a big advantage with patios. Regardless of the shape, size, and design of your home and yard, there's always room for a patio. A luxurious, full-service patio kitchen and adjoining eating area is great if you have the room and the budget, while a simple, stamped concrete slab is a cost-efficient way to add outdoor seating without taking up a lot of space.

A patio looks just as nice in front of the house as it does along the side or to the rear. Place it in front of entry doors to welcome guests, or build it in the back yard and surround it with plant life and running water for a natural setting. Install a patio around a swimming pool to expand the sitting area, or hide it in an isolated area for a private retreat.

Large patios that incorporate a number of features—such as brick pizza ovens, retaining walls, tiers of flowers, and water fountains—provide a wide range of decorative touches and comforts, but a patio can be simple and still serve your needs. Pathways or walkways that wind around the yard, a bench under an arbor, or a garden bed next to brick pavers can allow you to be creative while enjoying the outdoors to the fullest. Consider the patio a continual work in process. You can always add new plants, an overhead structure, and other amenities as your wants and needs evolve. Keep in mind that the more comfortable and enticing the patio is, the more it will draw people outside—whether it's for a planned party or a spontaneous get-together.

Patio Sites

Patios located in the front or side of the house have to look good from the street, where everyone passing by can see them. Keep the view open if you want to see and wave to neighbors as they pass by. Plant hedges or install a fence to provide privacy and reduce street noise.

Entry patios greet visitors and guide them to the house. These patios also liven up your front yard, making it an attractive place to socialize. If you don't have space at the front of the house for a patio, turn your driveway into one. Add a new surface, plant flowers along the border, and perhaps include a small retaining wall with foliage. A utilitarian driveway will instantly be transformed into a striking patio.

The area along the side of a house works well for pathways that connect the front and back yards, or for side-yard patios that offer comfortable sitting areas off the kitchen or living room.

An entry patio welcomes guests and leads them toward the house. Like most entry patios, this one is wide and includes landscaping along each side. The patio abuts the house, where steps lead to an entry door. There's plenty of room for seating and adding potted plants to make the area look more inviting. Keeping the patio open allows for an unobstructed view.

This driveway also serves as a patio. Stamped and decorative concrete are two options to soften the driveway's look, yet they're tough enough to handle vehicles. A patio driveway offers a warmer welcome than a cold slab of concrete or asphalt, which are typical driveway materials. This driveway patio is also well suited to planting along the edges.

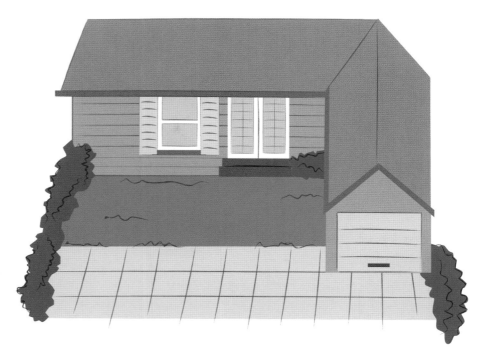

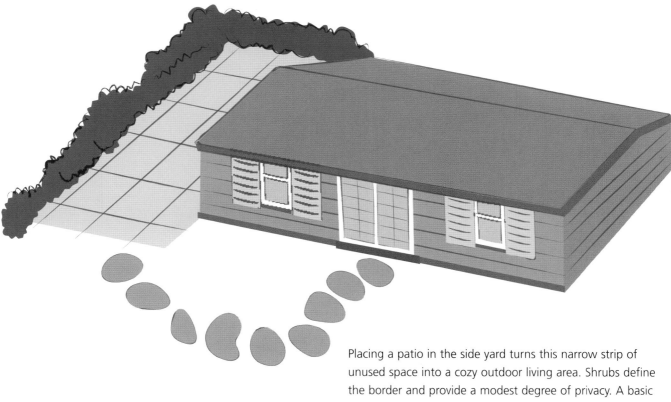

Placing a patio in the side yard turns this narrow strip of unused space into a cozy outdoor living area. Shrubs define the border and provide a modest degree of privacy. A basic stepping-stone path leads from the patio to the doors at the back of the house.

Patios that wrap inside or outside corners make the house seem larger and turn idle space into recreational areas. Install the patio around a single corner or extend it around the entire house.

For a more expansive patio, install your patio in the back yard. These patios take up as much or as little space as you let them and can incorporate a variety of materials and accessories. If you have a pool, surround it with a patio to add more space for sunbathing, barbecuing, and other activities.

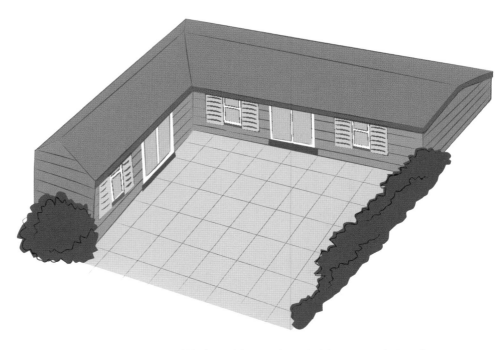

L- and U-shaped houses have inside corners that make excellent patio areas. This inside-corner patio spans two sides of the house, offering access from two sets of doors. Two sides of the patio are closed off by the house, adding a sense of privacy.

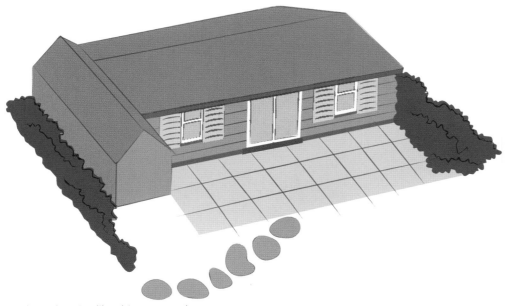

Back-yard patios like this one are the most popular type. They offer the most space since back yards typically make up the largest part of the property. A solid-surface patio next to the back of the house can give way to gardens, water features, or pathways.

Wraparound patios work especially well on flat lots that don't have much landscaping. The patio connects the front, side, and back yards, and can be accessed from any door to the house.

The focus of this pool-surround patio is undoubtedly the pool, but the patio gives the space more appeal and more room for activities other than swimming, like sun-tanning, reading, or cooking. Make sure the patio surface is slip resistant for swimmers getting in and out of the water.

Not all patios are attached to the house or at ground level. For a small lot where space is at a premium, place the patio on a balcony or rooftop and enhance it with potted trees and plants, as long as the structure can support the additional weight.

For yards with changing grades, multi-level patios tame the slopes with autonomous sections at various levels, tied together with stairs or walkways. Each section can serve a different purpose (for example, a cooking area on an upper level and a pool on the lower level), or the sections can work together, as they would with a multi-level garden.

To get away from the house completely, a detached patio is the answer. Locate it anywhere in the yard, perhaps for privacy or to relax in a natural setting.

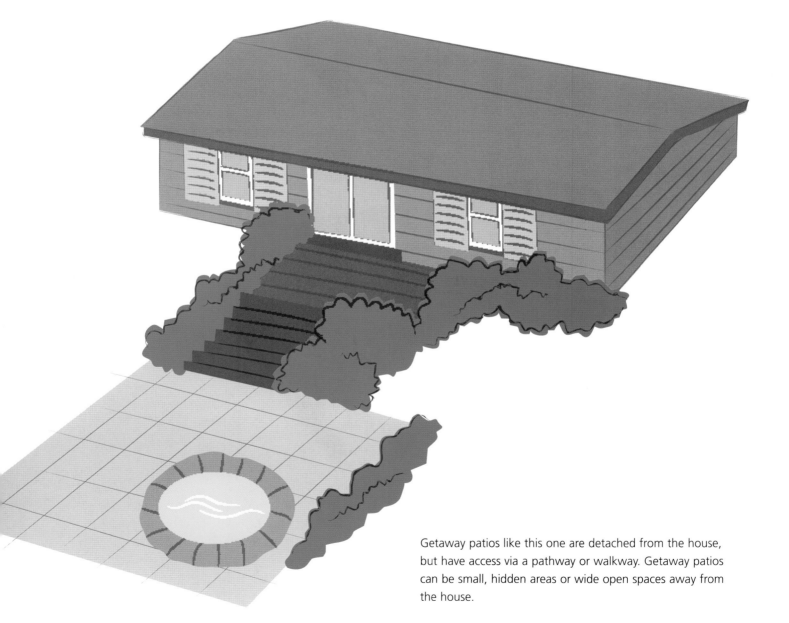

Getaway patios like this one are detached from the house, but have access via a pathway or walkway. Getaway patios can be small, hidden areas or wide open spaces away from the house.

The garage rooftop alongside this house makes a perfect location for a patio—there's ample room and a great view. A railing around the edge provides safety, and a few plants or accessories will personalize the space. The roof patio doesn't interfere with the landscape or consume valuable lawn space.

Different levels add character to this huge patio. The space near the house is perfect for barbecuing and outdoor dining, the middle level can be used for personal space, and the lower level has an inviting whirlpool.

Open Patios

Open-air patios are located with the sun in mind. You can watch the sunrise or witness a scenic sunset. They're also perfect when you want to bask in the sun's warmth or enjoy the fresh outdoor air. For many, the point of having a patio in the first place is to experience nature in as raw a form as possible. Place an umbrella or removable canopy on the patio, so you can block the sun if the heat gets too intense.

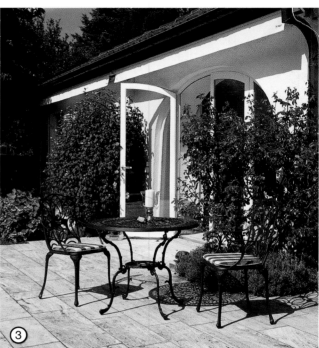

① Extending along the back of the house, this patio is large enough for a dining table and chairs as well as a more intimate setting next to the fireplace.

② This patio has an open, spacious feel as it extends away from the house and encircles the pool. Pool chairs and potted plants are spread out so the area isn't cluttered.

③ Strategically located to capture the sun, this patio doesn't have any interference from trees or overhangs. Double doors on the house open up to the patio to make the transition from indoor to outdoor space.

④ Although the sprawling patio is open to the elements, a basic folding umbrella is all that's needed to provide shade over the table.

⑤ Wrapping around two sides of the house, this narrow patio allows everyone to soak up the sun throughout the day.

⑥ A short wall and trees line the edges of this concrete patio, yet there's nothing closing off the overhead view.

⑦ Due to their immense size, patios that surround pools are often left open. Here, shade is provided by trees growing alongside the water's edge.

Closed Patios

Closed patios are at least partly shaded, so the sun's heat and glare won't drive you inside. These patios aren't necessarily boxed in on all four sides, but they do have some type of cover overhead. Extending eaves, building overhead structures, and installing awnings are all popular ways to enclose the patio and block the sun and rain. The patio surface usually extends out into the open so you can move into the sun if you want to.

① This second-story deck leaves plenty of room underneath for a concrete patio. At the same time, the deck encloses almost the entire patio structure.

② An overhead deck is a natural structure for closing off part of this patio. The table-and-chair set is positioned in the deck's shade near the house.

③ The balcony proved to be an ideal spot for this patio, which overlooks the ocean. The patio nook is enclosed on three sides and overhead.

④ This patio, partly enclosed and partly open, is conveniently located beneath a deck. Finished decking keeps out the rain.

⑤ Although the overhead structure here isn't watertight, it creates a slatted ceiling for the patio.

⑥ This patio is closed off overhead, but natural sunlight can reach the seating area.

Patio Surfaces

As the most visible part of the patio, the flooring sets the tone. Some surfaces, including brick and stone, give the patio a formal appeal, while others, such as colorful concrete and loose materials, give it an informal look. Plan the materials you want to use, and then decide which design you want them to create. Decide if you want straight lines, in which case you may wish to use brick or concrete, or if you want random lines, such as those created by irregular stones.

① This mosaic butterfly adds a quirky touch to the patio. It sets a playful tone and works well with the colorful flowers.

② Stone-filled joints break up this pool-side concrete patio into smaller sections, giving the intersecting lines a different color and texture.

③ Here, concrete steps connect a stone patio on the lower level to a stone pathway on the upper level. Pebbles give the patio an informal look.

④ These sleek pebble-dash tiles provide an ideal setting for modern design and contemporary furniture.

⑤ Vintage-look bricks give this patio a rustic appeal. Bricks like this can make a patio and walkway look decades old, even when they're brand new.

⑥ A continuous, uninterrupted surface gives this patio a classy look, making the area appear as one large, outdoor room rather than several individual sections tied together.

⑦ The neutral colors of this stone surface don't compete with the pool, which is the focal point.

Brick Patio Patterns

Brick patterns, called "bonds," range from simple to intricate. They can create a subtle design or become the focal point of the patio. Some patterns work best for covering large, square surfaces, while others enhance small areas or irregularly shaped patios.

For example, the simplistic elegance of the basketweave works well on large patios while the straight lines in the running bond pattern makes small or narrow areas appear larger. Angled brick arrangements in the herringbone patterns lend themselves to patios with unusual shapes or those with attached walkways.

① Basketweave
② Basketweave variation
③ Half basketweave
④ Flemish bond
⑤ Herringbone with stack bond detail
⑥ Herringbone
⑦ Pinwheel
⑧ Stack bond
⑨ Diagonal herringbone
⑩ Jack on Jack
⑪ Running bond
⑫ Circular design

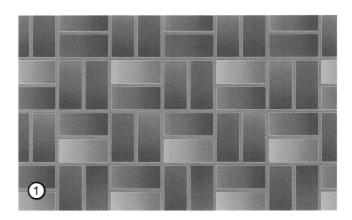

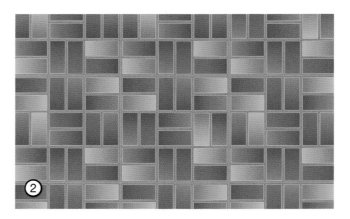

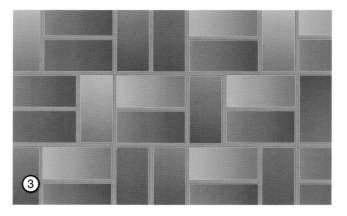

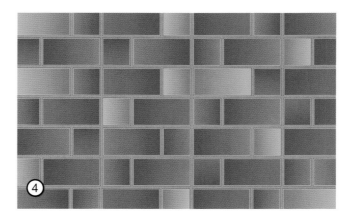

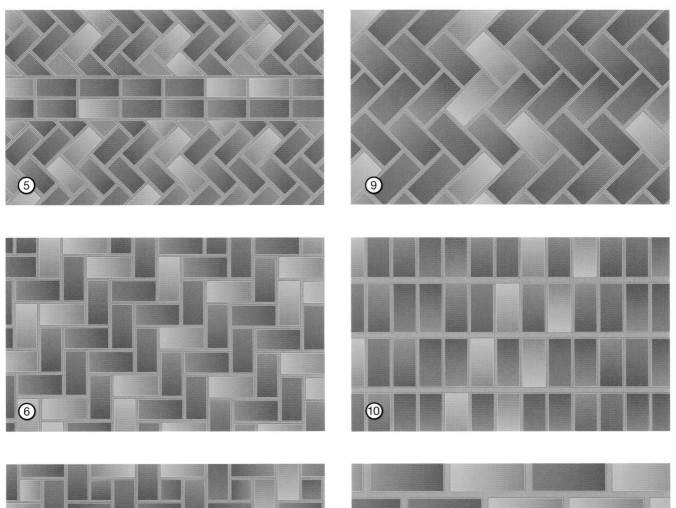

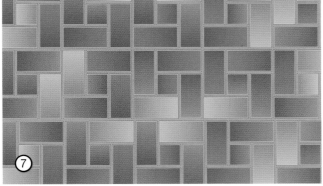

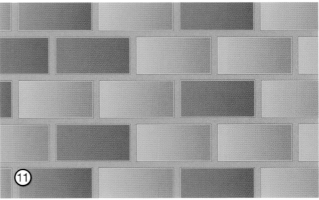

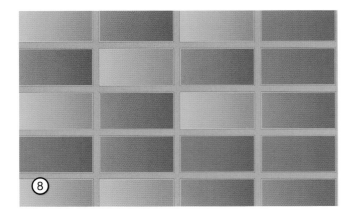

Stairs

It's lovely to be able to open a patio door, walk down a few stairs, then step onto a great-looking patio. Stairs play a prominent role by connecting different sections of multi-level patios, connecting patios to entry doors, or connecting patios to overhead decks.

Concrete steps are popular and match almost any patio décor, while stone and brick are sometimes used for short runs of stairs on tiered patios. Railings can provide well-defined accents with colorful or decorative rails or spindles, which help offset monotone stairs.

① These warm red stairs match the exterior of the house. Small, multi-colored flowerpots mark the edges.

② This elegant, winding staircase becomes a focal point for the luxury patio. The bright railings complement the stone steps.

③ A dual staircase allows access to either side of this paved area, so utilities on both sides are easy to reach. Each step has its own light.

④ Placing a metal band on the edge of each stair keeps the concrete from chipping here as well as adding an ornamental touch.

⑤ Flagstone has been used in the construction of this patio, the stairs, and the retaining wall in the background, so they all match.

⑥ Clean, sharp lines define this patio, and carry over to the stairs. The tempered-glass stair railings are transparent so they don't interrupt the look of the concrete.

⑦ Ornamental railings characterize these curved stairs. The pole helps to support their weight.

Edgings

Edgings are more than accents surrounding a patio. They may also serve a functional purpose, namely holding loose patio materials, such as gravel or wood chips, firmly in place. Edgings also soften the change from the patio to the yard. You can make the transition subtle, by using the same material for both the patio and the edging, or bold, using a totally different material for contrast. There are many edging options. Certain materials suit some patio shapes better than others. Brick, for example, works well only along straight lines or very gradual curves, while concrete and plastic edging can wrap around any shape.

① These brick pavers follow the gentle, carefree contour of the patio. The mortar between the bricks matches the patio surface, tying everything together for a unified look.

② A generous concrete strip clearly defines the edge of this patio and looks similar to the grout lines in between the tiles.

③ Set vertically in the ground along the perimeter of the patio, these brick edgings, called "sailors," match the patio materials for a clean transition from patio to yard.

④ Tilting the vertically installed bricks at an angle gives this edging an interesting visual effect.

⑤ Incredibly thin, the plastic edging here is almost invisible and defers attention to the interlocking pavers on the patio.

⑥ Timber edgings add a rustic element to patios. Here, short wooden posts have been driven into the ground to form a base. Timber planks are laid lengthways on top and nailed in place for a finished look.

⑦ Large rocks or boulders partially buried around the patio can double as landscaping elements. These edgings work especially well if there are other boulders in the yard.

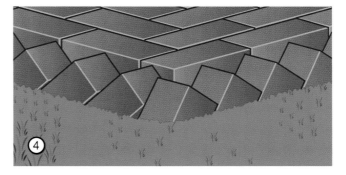

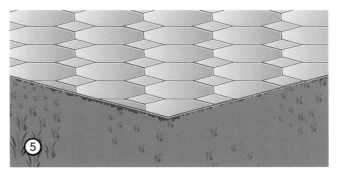

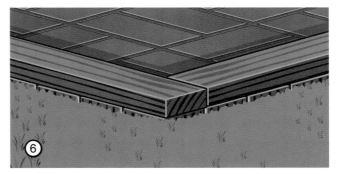

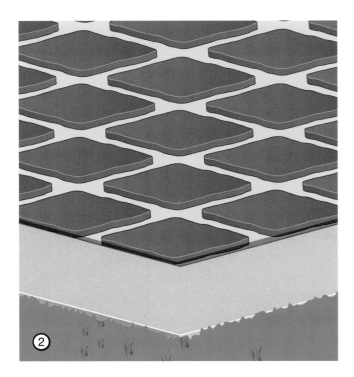

Retaining Walls

Retaining walls are ideal in sloping yards where you want to hold back the soil for a level patio. Place the retaining wall at the bottom of a slope and fill in the back side with rich soil to provide a perfect garden bed for flowers; or use the wall to create a multi-level patio that turns the yard into tiers.

Brick, stone, concrete, or wood can all make a handsome retaining wall. Alternatively, give the wall a smooth coating and paint it to match other elements in the house or yard.

① An upper-level patio sits on one end of the retaining wall, while a lower-level pool with sundeck is on the other. The wide capstone on top of the wall gives it a finished look.

② Tall, substantial, and brightly painted, this retaining wall serves aesthetic and functional roles. It matches the modern furniture while supporting the foliage above.

③ A giant retaining wall near the house allows for a lower-level patio, waterfall, and pool. A second wall near the patio supports a flower garden.

④ Made out of the same stone as the patio, the retaining wall replicates the organic curves of the pool and patio.

⑤ Three levels of stone retaining wall add several tiers to this stunning patio. The same stone is also used in the pool fence posts.

Pathways and Walkways

Pathways, or walkways, help to connect areas in your yard or to direct traffic through your outdoor space. Let the path meander for a leisurely look, or curve it in a pattern that replicates other elements in the yard, such as a circular patio or water garden.

Construct your pathway with the same material as the patio surface for consistency, or simply place stepping stones at intervals and let grass grow between them for an authentic natural feel. Either option is preferable to trampling the grass for a makeshift pathway.

① Enormous slabs of stone that match the patio surface are spaced close enough for easy movement along this walkway, but they're far enough apart to let plants grow around them.

② A pathway leading from the patio guides people through this dense garden. It provides a convenient place to walk without crushing plants.

③ Flagstones with mortared joints make up this narrow path that spans the yard. A wooden railing running alongside makes the pathway seem like a bridge.

④ This wide pathway patio, composed of large smooth stones, leads through a vine-covered arbor.

⑤ The brick pathway here cuts across the manicured lawn with a slight curve, giving it an attractive twist. Stepping stones beside the gazebo lead into the woods.

Borders

Install a border around your patio to clearly define the boundaries. A border is an easy way to separate the patio from the rest of the yard or from the neighbor's property. The border doesn't have to be a continuous structure. Trees regularly spaced along the periphery define the border without closing off the entire view. Borders don't have to be tall either. Knee-high masonry walls or plants encircling the patio mark the border and leave the view open. To make a bold statement and isolate the patio, use a privacy fence or a wall as the border.

① Waist-high foliage divides the patio, separating the eating area from the rest of the space. A masonry retaining wall curves along the patio edge to mark the border.

② A tall stone wall with mortared joints serves as a border along the back of the patio, while a two-block-high masonry wall marks the border along the sides.

③ Layers of flowers are a fitting border for the stone patio. The outermost edge of shrubs is cut at a uniform height.

④ Several borders surround the patio. Potted plants act as the first tier, followed by a mid-sized concrete wall, followed by tall, slender plants that provide almost total privacy.

⑤ Ceramic pots with plants in front of manicured hedges, with a steel fence behind them, provide a triple border for this stone patio.

⑥ A line of trees borders the side of the patio, while the house abuts the patio and naturally borders the front end.

Fences

Fences serve a range of functions—from offering privacy and providing security to keeping kids on the patio and blocking the wind. You have a lot of fence options. Wood has long been the favorite material, though maintenance-free fences such as aluminum and vinyl are gaining in popularity. You can also go for a "living" fence by planting hedges or bushes along your fence row.

Fences can follow the grade of the yard and stay close to the ground, or step down in sections, which keeps the top of the fence level but can leave large gaps between the fence and the ground.

① Fences are required around most swimming pools, and the slender railings in this fence provide the needed security without obstructing the view.

② Red roses intertwine with the wood-lattice fence to form a colorful mix. Lattice is the ideal railing system to encourage roses to grow. The roses will eventually take over the entire fence.

③ A trellis installed behind these planters provides a surface for the climbing vines to cling to as they grow. A large section of fencing with vertical railings offers a nice variation over the short brick wall.

④ Lights attached to these fence posts illuminate the patio at night. The unpainted slats have a raw look.

⑤ Lattice fencing can look fancy, like on this flowery patio. Rounding the top and incorporating a circular design in the middle fence section, as well as adding decorative caps, turns a simple fence into a classy structure.

⑥ A metal fence atop this brick wall encloses the patio without closing off the view. A cactus garden at the base of the wall adds further color and interest.

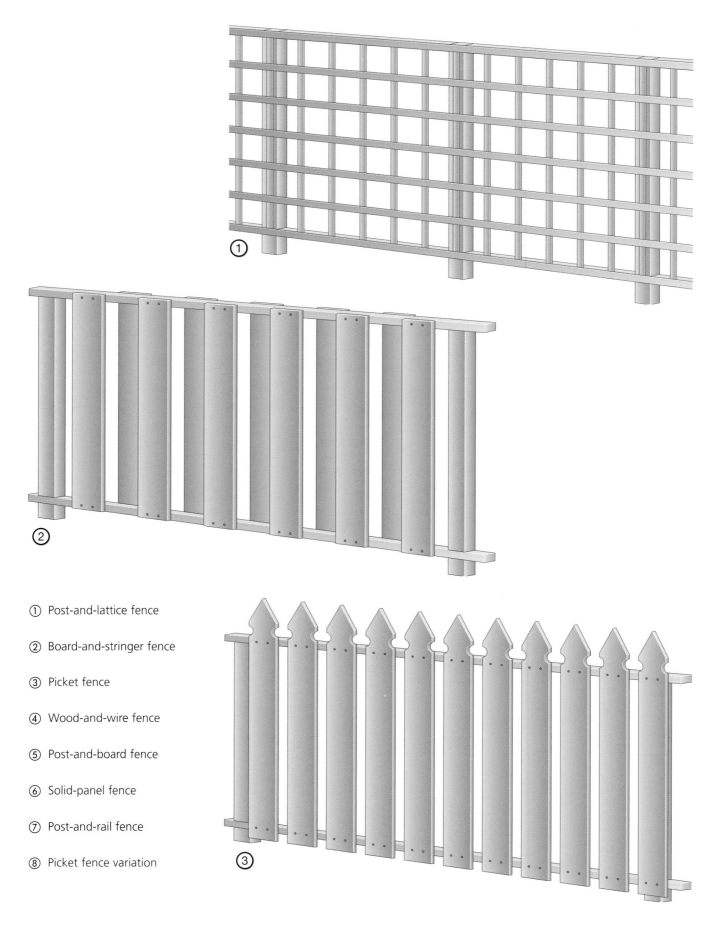

① Post-and-lattice fence

② Board-and-stringer fence

③ Picket fence

④ Wood-and-wire fence

⑤ Post-and-board fence

⑥ Solid-panel fence

⑦ Post-and-rail fence

⑧ Picket fence variation

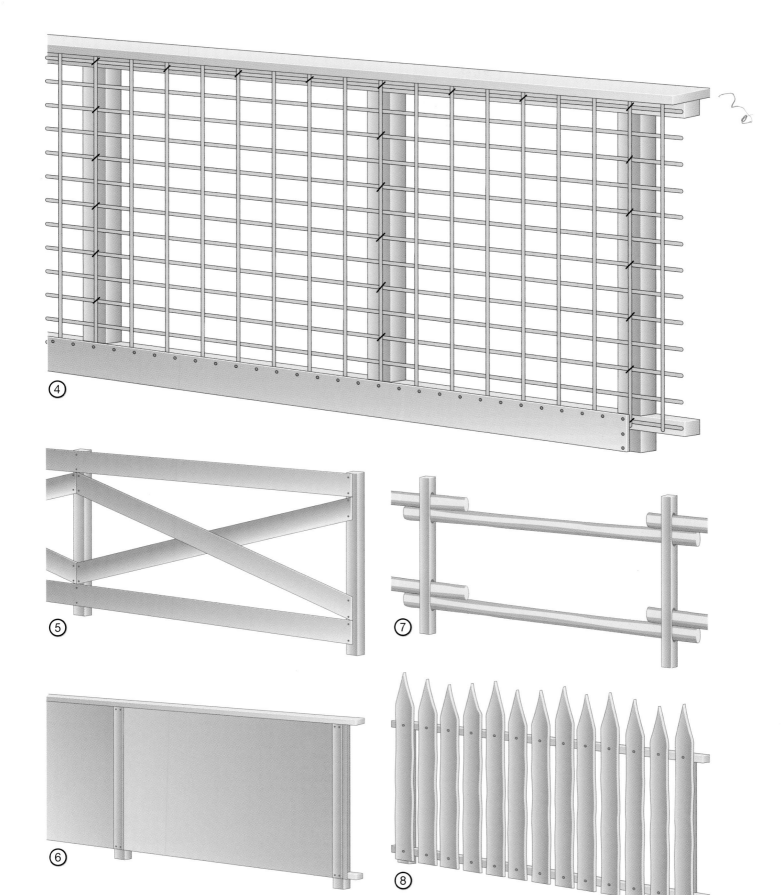

Walls

Patio walls are typically built of masonry, and placed along one or more sides of the patio for privacy, protection from the wind, or decoration. Make sure you plan to build your structure in the correct position for serving your particular purpose. If you want to liven up a wall, cover it with ivy or climbing plants. Incorporate your wall or walls into the patio by using the same colors, materials, or accents used elsewhere.

① The wall along the front of this patio is short enough to hold potted plants, while the wall along the back is taller for privacy and security. The wall's earth-brown color is picked up in the ceramic pots and the patio furniture.

② Ambient lighting emphasizes the inset designs on this wall, giving it a three-dimensional look. A solid backdrop shelters the seating area from wind.

③ Tall, smooth walls surround this patio for total privacy and wind protection. The bases of the built-in tables and seats are painted to match the walls. The throw cushions are also the same warm color.

④ Tall white walls completely enclose this back-yard patio. Narrow slats of vertical and horizontal wood provide a makeshift trellis for the climbing vine.

⑤ Hundreds of stones are stacked together to create this curved wall. The structure separates the concrete patio from the woods on the other side.

⑥ Slender trees soften the solidity of this wall. Loose gravel borders the patio, forming a kind of stone garden.

⑦ Blocking the view of neighboring houses, this very high wall isolates the patio from its surroundings, reduces outside noise, and helps to block most direct sunlight.

Masonry walls are either built with mortar, which is the most common construction method and required for tall walls, or dry stacked, which means the bricks or stones are simply placed on top of each other without mortar. In domestic settings dry-stacked walls are usually limited to about knee-height and sometimes have soil placed behind them to keep them from tipping over. Decide if you want brick or stone of uniform size for parallel lines on the wall, or if you want random shapes and sizes that eliminate straight lines.

① Red clay brick with mortar
② Cobblestone brick with mortar
③ Irregular stones set in mortar
④ Light-colored stone block
⑤ Dark stone with a standard size
⑥ Colored stone in random sizes
⑦ Dry-stacked stone
⑧ Rock and stone in mortar
⑨ Flat stone in mortar
⑩ Dry-stacked flat stone
⑪ Dry-stacked stone in irregular shapes
⑫ Flagstone wall with tight joints

5

9

6

10

7

11

8

12

Gardens

Whether it's a narrow border of greenery or a blossoming oasis of flowers, a garden is an essential part of a patio. Gardens bring colorful, fragrant plants into the outdoor space, which in turn attract butterflies and birds. A vegetable or herb garden nearby is also a welcome addition. A garden can fit anywhere you have soil, so you probably have enough space for one. Tending to your plants will turn into an enjoyable hobby that doesn't require expert gardening skills.

① Tiny gardens are built into this pool-side patio, effectively mixing plants with the stone surface. A larger garden is also located behind the pool.

② Lush gardens encircle this back-yard patio. Unobtrusive benches provide seating nooks where people can enjoy the tropical look and feel.

③ Bushes and shrubs grow in the garden along the edge of this cobblestone patio, while flowers and saplings grow in pots beside the house.

④ Several sizes, colors, and types of plants make this garden the focal point of the outdoor room. The dense foliage also provides privacy.

⑤ Filling the space between the driveway and sidewalk, the garden here makes effective use of the narrow strip of yard. The garden follows the rounded shape of the driveway as well as the straight lines of the sidewalk and adjoining patio edges.

⑥ Enough space was left between the patio and the retaining walls here for a border garden. Plants are also incorporated in the soil behind the walls and in the raised garden bed next to the pool.

Raised Garden Beds

Built above the ground, raised garden beds can be any shape, any size, and can go anywhere on your patio. Because the beds are filled with enriched soil, they offer a perfect environment for flowers. Raised garden beds are often used in conjunction with retaining walls, which can also hold soil. Flagstone and wood are both effective materials for building raised beds.

① Brightly painted, multi-tiered garden beds give this patio a greater sense of dimension and repeat the layered theme in the sunken patio surface. Raised beds along the right side balance out the patio.

② Building raised garden beds around this patio has enclosed it in "living" walls.

③ Raised garden beds are ideal for alpine plants and rock gardens, as they have good drainage. This circular alpine bed provides a calm focal point in the otherwise featureless paved yard.

④ A vertically installed wooden skirt emphasizes the height of these garden beds, which wrap around the patio edge.

⑤ This garden bed isn't very tall, but it's raised enough to be separate from the patio surface and offer a place for the plants to take root. Wide capstones on the garden-bed walls give the structure a finished look.

Patios with Decks

Combining a patio with a deck gives you the best of both worlds—a raised structure for impressive views, and a ground-level area that puts you in touch with gardens, pools, or play areas. An overhead deck can provide shelter from the sun and rain for a patio underneath, while a patio adjoining a deck affords space for elements, such as water fountains or garden beds, that won't fit on the deck. Plan the space so that the deck and patio interact in a coherent way, with convenient access between the two.

① Here, a wooden deck with an adjoining gazebo overlooks the shapely pool, while a patio leads right to the water.

② This outdoor space has almost every feature you could ask for: a raised deck with glass rails, a gazebo for shelter, a multi-level patio with a built-in garden, a hot tub, and a pool!

③ A ground-level deck under the awning provides a shaded escape from the sun, then gives way to a pool-surround patio.

④ Connected to the house with access from the back door, this deck serves as the primary gathering place. The patio and walking path along the side of the deck conform to the deck shape.

⑤ This raised deck is connected to the patio by a flight of stairs. The deck is used for entertaining. The patio offers flowers, a water fountain, and a garden bench.

Deck Materials

It's surprising how many materials there are for decks. Most people naturally think of wood when they think of decks since wood has been the predominant material for centuries. But even in the wood category, there are a lot of choices. Redwood offers a rich appearance. Cedar has an attractive wood grain. Treated lumber is less expensive, but not as good-looking. If you don't want to deal with adding a fresh coat of stain or paint every few years, there are maintenance-free options. Wood composites mimic the look of real wood, but never need upkeep. Vinyl has a sleek plastic look that cleans easily with water.

Natural wood is a popular option for decks because of its warmth, beauty, and rich color tones. The drawback to wood is regular maintenance, such as stripping and staining, and the wood can splinter and rot. If you want a maintenance-free alternative to wood, choose vinyl or composite materials. These have proven reliable, and they are available in several attractive colors and designs. Even better, they never need painting or staining, and the decking doesn't warp or crack.

Decide how you'll stain or paint your deck. That'll help you to choose the material. If you want to paint the surface, go with an inexpensive wood species, like treated lumber or a knotty wood, since the surface will be covered anyway. If you plan to use a transparent or semi-transparent stain, or just use a wood sealant—all of which highlight the wood grain—then go with a high-quality wood like redwood or cedar. You can also combine paint and stain on the deck. Consider staining the deck boards and painting the railings a bright color to draw attention.

If you want color options but want to avoid paint, consider a solid stain. These stains offer vibrant colors that penetrate the wood and also protect against damaging sun rays. They also emphasize the wood grain, rather than covering it like paint does. To capture the natural color of wood, use a clear sealant, which protects the surface from the sun.

Opposite: This cozy deck comes to life with white balusters arranged in a sunrise pattern, a white pergola overhead, and flowers growing in pots and in the bench planter.

Right: Decking installed in an angular pattern intersects where the upper deck steps down to the lower deck, creating a chevron pattern.

Redwood

Redwood has been a popular wood for decks for decades, especially in California where the redwood trees grow. The wood is more expensive than most, but it has a warm, rich look that's unique to the species. Several grades of redwood are available in different price ranges. Redwood has an attractive grain and it is resistant to shrinking, so the deck continues to look good over the years. The wood contains little or no pitch or resins, so it holds stains well.

① Long redwood boards work well on this large, angular shaped deck.

② A solid stain gives this redwood deck a deep, reddish-brown color.

③ Luxuriant redwood is used throughout the deck and pergola, giving the space a warm look and feel.

④ Dark-stained redwood decking, including the raised octagonal section, matches the redwood cap over the white painted railing.

⑤ White painted accessories, in this case the pergola, and accents, like the railing posts, offer a complementary color scheme with the redwood decking.

⑥ Including a simple decoration in the middle balusters gives the deck character and fits nicely with the wood-crafted posts.

⑦ The redwood decking under the area rug and dining set makes this deck look almost like a formal dining room.

Cedar

Cedar is gaining a reputation as a nice-looking, less expensive alternative to redwood. Cedar has a straight wood grain that not only makes the decking look appealing, but it helps keep the lumber straight so it doesn't cup or warp.

Cedar is naturally resistant to decay and insect damage, which means the decking will last a long time. The wood also works well with any architectural style, from classic to modern, so it will fit any deck and look good next to any house.

① Using a sealant rather than a stain lets the true beauty of the cedar shine through on the deck.

② The colorful wood grain gives this cedar deck a lavish look that's easy to fall in love with.

③ A clear stain brings out the natural warmth of cedar here. It's a finish that goes well with any house siding.

④ Routed posts with mitered tops and an intriguing angled design on the top of the railings give this cedar deck an extraordinary appearance.

⑤ A semi-transparent stain helps this cedar deck and pergola maintain their true colors, yet protects the wood from the sun.

⑥ Using cedar for the deck rails, skirting, built-in planter, and gazebo helps tie the separate structures together for a unified facade.

Treated Lumber

Treated lumber, also called pressure-treated or green lumber because of its color, is treated with preservatives to keep the wood from rotting when it's in contact with or close to the ground. Most decks have some treated lumber, usually for the posts, beams, and joists. You can also use treated lumber for decking. It's less expensive than most other woods, and it's a good choice for decks built on or near the ground. Treated lumber is highly corrosive, so special fasteners are needed to withstand the elements over time.

① Treated lumber and metal railings make the deck solid, and they also look good together.

② Pressure-treated lumber generally isn't used for railings, which is why these railings are made with metal and vinyl.

③ Since parts of the deck, including the stairs and skirting, are in direct contact with the ground, treated lumber is used to ensure the wood won't rot. Paint gives the deck a handsome finish.

④ Long boards are used to avoid breaks in this decking, giving the surface a continuous flow. The treated lumber is painted to match the railing posts.

⑤ Painted white to match the house and outdoor furniture, the deck stands out amidst the greenery growing along each side.

⑥ Treated hem-fir decking holds up well in this wooded environment and lets some of its natural grain show through.

Vinyl

Vinyl offers a sleek, plastic-looking deck surface that will never need maintenance, other than an occasional washing off with the hose. Vinyl works great as a pool surround since people walking barefoot won't have to worry about splinters. And the surface isn't as slippery as many stone finishes.

Almost all vinyl decking uses an installation system that hides the fasteners, like a tongue-and-groove system. Likewise, interconnecting rails hide fasteners in the railings. Several colors of vinyl are available, though white and tan are the most prevalent shades.

① Shiny white vinyl decking and posts join with black metal rails for a contrasting color scheme that comes out perfectly.

② Vinyl steps provide deck access along one side of the pathway. The vinyl decking is laid in an angular pattern to align with the stair side of the deck.

③ This vinyl decking looks similar to wood, but without the worry of splinters.

④ The gray coloring of this deck cuts down on the bright, shiny look associated with vinyl. It also interacts well with the masonry stairs.

⑤ Ideally situated in the shade of nearby trees, this tan-colored vinyl deck fits the style of the house while offering wide access to the yard.

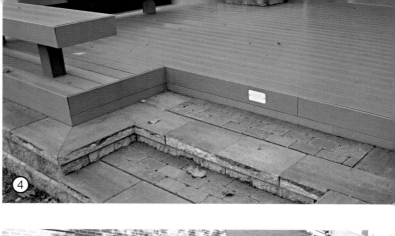

Composites

Usually made of wood fibers and plastics, composite decking is designed to look like wood, complete with imitation wood-textured grain. But unlike wood, it won't splinter, rot, or warp, and it never needs a finish. It also resists termites. Some composite boards are solid all the way through, while others are hollow or ribbed. The decking is strong and holds up well over time. Various colors of composite decking are available, so you can get the color you want without having to bother with painting or staining.

④

⑤

⑥

① Including real wood on the deck, like the pergola, deck posts, and skirting, makes the composite decking look even more like authentic wood.

② Here, composite decking boards are installed in different patterns to create interest. A different-colored composite border is placed along the outside of the deck for contrast.

③ A soft curve in this deck is repeated and enlarged in the steps, all of which are made with composite materials.

④ Composite materials make intermixing different colors on the deck easy, such as the decking border and stair-tread trim shown here.

⑤ The raised deck, stairs, and landing here could all pass for painted wood, but they are actually built with a tan composite material.

⑥ This composite deck has a subtle curve along the front edge that provides more space for the table-and-chair set.

Finishes, Stains, and Paints

Finishes, stains, and paints are easy to apply to wood decks. Apply them a month or two after the deck is built, giving time for the wood to dry out, then every two to four years after that. Finishes, stains, and paints make your deck last longer by protecting against rotting, mildew, and decay. They also help protect against scuffmarks and spills that could otherwise stain the wood.

The second benefit is aesthetics. A sealant, stain, or paint gives the wood an attractive finish, whether it's a vibrant paint that matches the house's exterior, a rich stain that enhances the look of the deck, or a nearly invisible sealant that captures the natural look of the wood.

① The decking and rails on this deck are finished with a deep-brown stain, while the railing posts and bottom rails are painted white. The stain and paint give the deck an attractive two-tone color scheme.

② All of the deck elements—the decking, built-in bench, and stairs—are painted brown, which gives the deck a finish that blends in well with the bricks on the house.

③ White paint is the perfect choice for the deck railing and overhead pergola here because it draws the eye upward and provides a sleek, clean look against the gray accent.

④ A rich red-brown stain gives this deck a warm appearance and stands out against the pale house siding and the pool.

⑤ The platform deck and the furniture here are both in neutral shades, which allow the flower accents to shine.

⑥ This tan stain clearly defines the deck's borders and helps make the deck the focal point of the back yard.

Clear finishes are non-pigmented sealers formulated to protect against the elements, such as water and the sun's ultraviolet rays, without changing the wood's color. Properly applied, a clear finish will repel water.

Clear finishes seal the wood and prevent mildew, and they also slow down the weathering process, helping to preserve the wood's natural color. However, even with a clear finish, the wood will eventually weather. Cedar will turn a silver gray, and redwood will turn a dark gray. The finishes are available with a water or oil base.

① Untreated redwood
② All heart redwood with a clear finish
③ Redwood with a clear finish
④ Heart redwood with a clear finish
⑤ B-grade redwood with a clear finish
⑥ Garden-grade redwood with a clear finish
⑦ Untreated cedar
⑧ Architect cedar with a clear finish
⑨ Custom cedar with a clear finish
⑩ Architect knotty cedar with a clear finish
⑪ Custom knotty cedar with a clear finish
⑫ Seasoned cedar with a clear finish

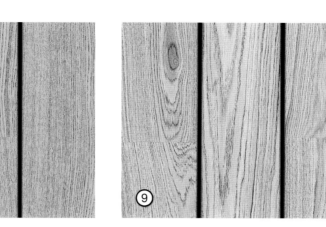

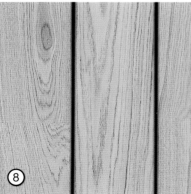

Stains are pigmented finishes that penetrate the wood, protecting it against water and sunlight. Solid stains contain more pigment, resulting in a deeper finish than semi-transparent versions.

Stains won't affect the wood texture or grain, but they will enhance or change the wood's color. Stains are available in wood-tone colors, like browns and reds, that match the wood's natural color. Be aware that the color of the stain will change depending on the type of wood species on the deck. All stains in the gallery pages 116 to 123 are applied to cedar.

① Olivewood
② Seashore gray
③ Chestnut brown
④ Woodland brown
⑤ Brownish gray
⑥ Natural cedar
⑦ Natural redwood
⑧ Charcoal gray
⑨ Sand dune
⑩ Autumn brown
⑪ Terra-cotta brown
⑫ Fawn brown
⑬ Frosted maple
⑭ Red cedar
⑮ Saddle brown
⑯ Slate gray
⑰ Natural oak
⑱ Dark red cedar
⑲ Black walnut
⑳ Moss green

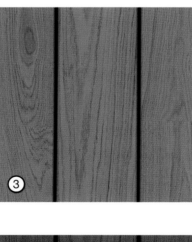

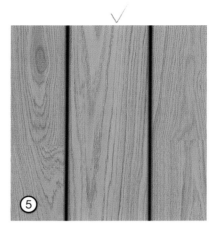

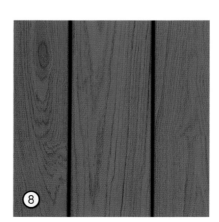

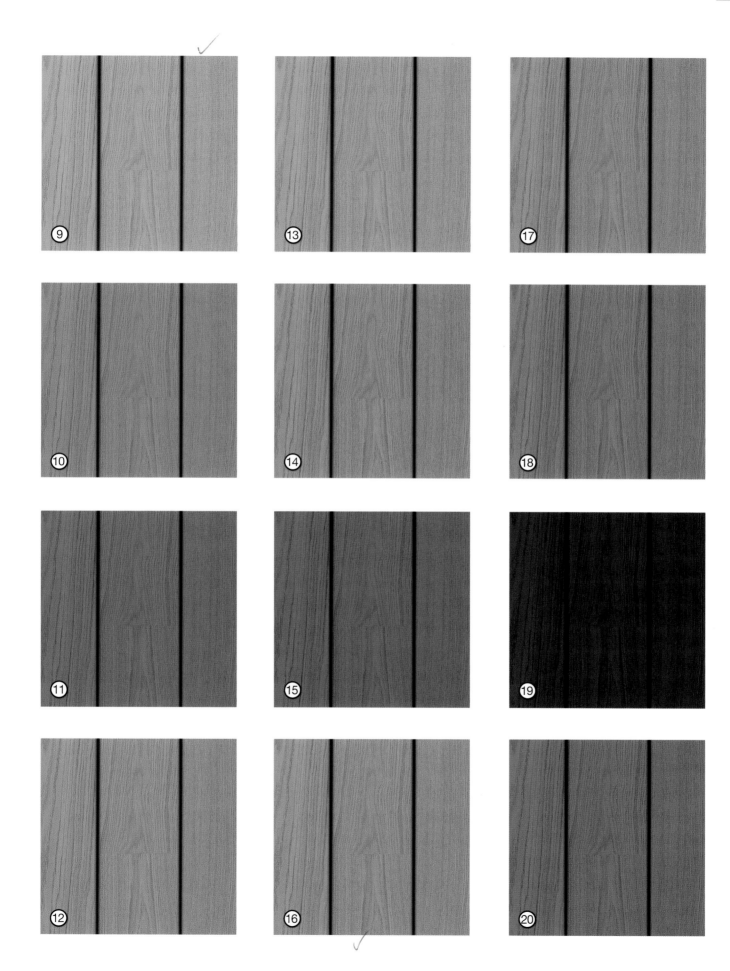

Solid color stains, also called "opaque stains," are no longer limited to semi-transparent shades of brown; they are now available in nearly every imaginable shade. Stains provide a rich color that can complement the décor of any house. Unlike many clear sealants, colored stains protect against damaging ultraviolet rays from the sun. And unlike paints that form a film and sit on top of the surface, stains penetrate into the wood, so they will not crack and peel as the wood expands and contracts.

① White
② Slate blue
③ Cedar
④ Chocolate
⑤ Antique gray
⑥ Tan
⑦ Brick
⑧ Beechwood
⑨ Mulberry
⑩ Coffee
⑪ Light khaki
⑫ Sandy taupe
⑬ Autumn brown
⑭ Espresso
⑮ Prairie dust
⑯ Sahara gray
⑰ Hickory brown
⑱ Shamrock green
⑲ Medium brown
⑳ Pewter gray

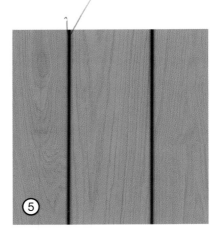

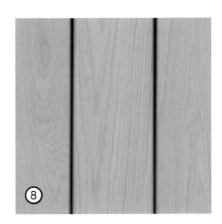

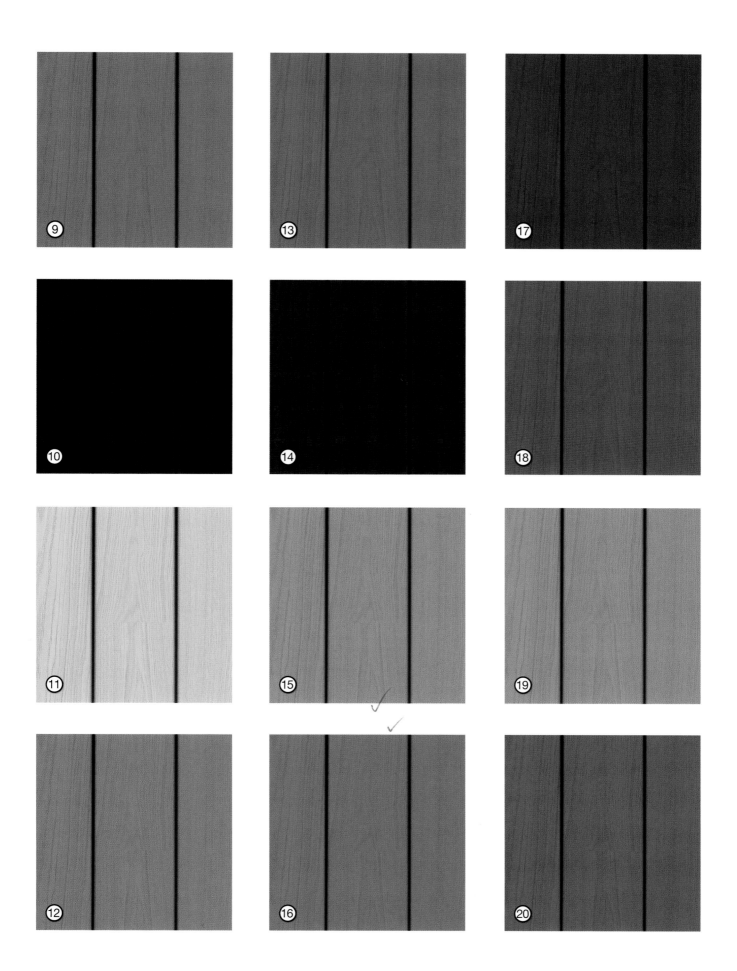

Continued from page 118.

Solid stains conceal the wood grain, which hides minor flaws, but still allows some of the texture to come through. Stains are a good finish to use when the decking is knotty or blemished, has an unattractive grain, or when the wood is an unsuitable color. These stains are available in both latex and oil-based types and can be used on previously stained wood. Solid stains contain more pigment than semi-transparent stains, they are fade resistant, and they leave a flat finish that's water-repellent. Most solid stains are also mildew resistant.

① Canyon brown
② Golden brown
③ Olive
④ Shale
⑤ Light-brown sugar
⑥ Pear
⑦ Blue gray
⑧ Graphite gray
⑨ Birch wood
⑩ Slate blue
⑪ Mallard green
⑫ Taupe gray
⑬ Ivory
⑭ Wave crest
⑮ Misty gray
⑯ Cerulean blue
⑰ Sea green
⑱ Spruce green
⑲ Stone
⑳ Steel blue

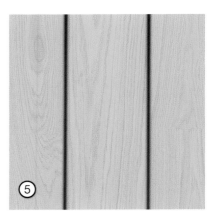
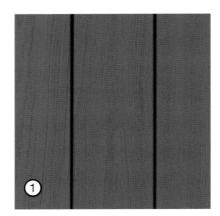
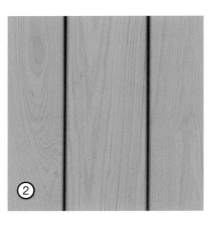
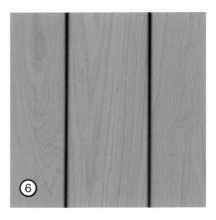

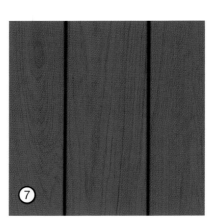
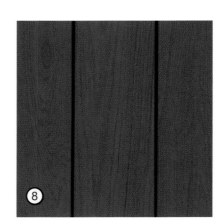

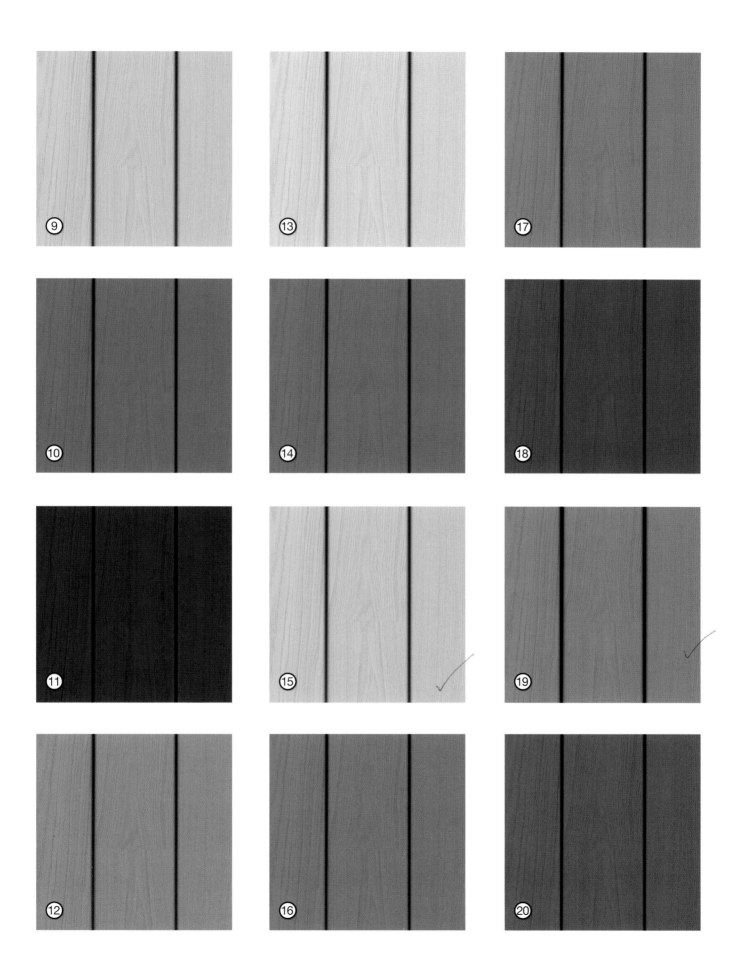

Continued from page 120.

Solid stains are brushed onto the deck in the same way as traditional stains. Like traditional stains, they'll get darker with each coat, so it's important to apply a single, even coat and avoid going over the same area more than once. Staining an area that's already finished will leave dark marks wherever the stain overlaps. Primers are recommended before applying some solid stains for a smooth, uniform finish. Solid stains should last four years on heavily traveled decks, six years on less frequently used decks, and six years on the railings.

① Blackened gray
② Stone gray
③ Traditional cedar
④ Russet
⑤ Forest dew
⑥ Traditional gray
⑦ Taupe
⑧ Traditional mahogany
⑨ Oxford brown
⑩ Dark gray
⑪ Redwood
⑫ Slate gray
⑬ Traditional coffee
⑭ Colonial yellow
⑮ Glacier blue
⑯ Beige
⑰ Navajo red
⑱ Spruce blue
⑲ Evergreen
⑳ Ultra-white

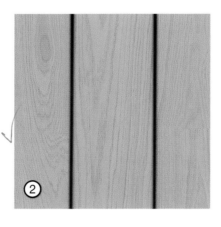

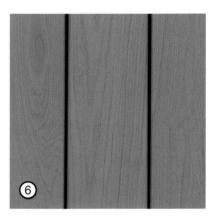

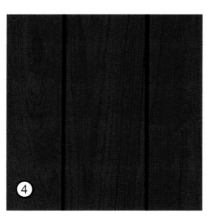

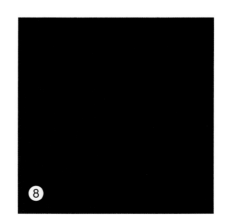

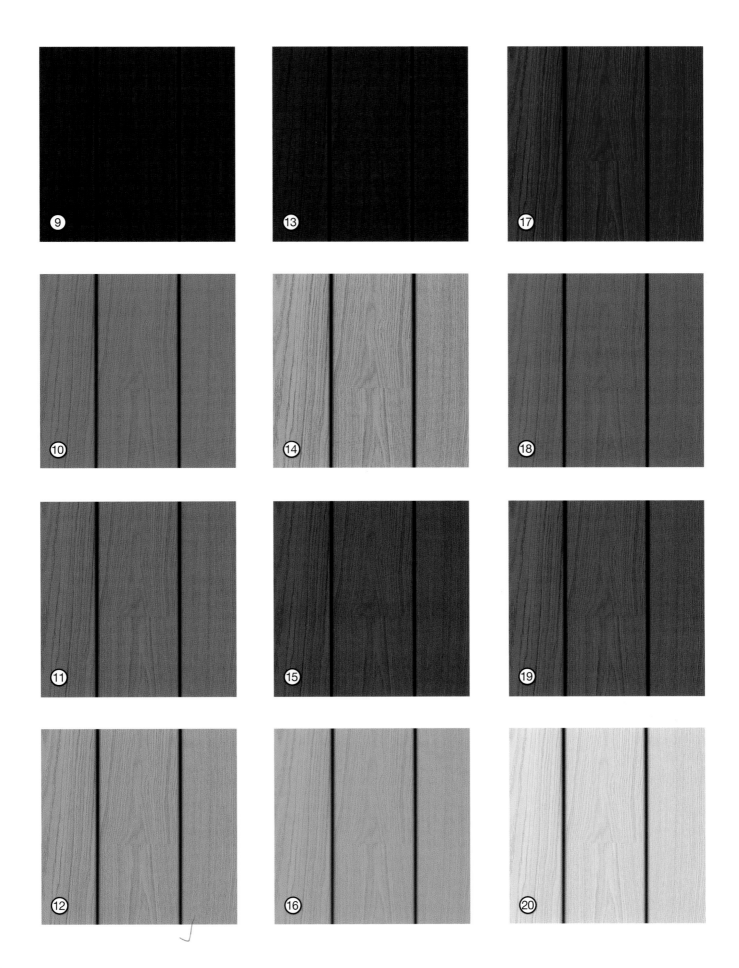

Paint is available in a seemingly endless number of colors, giving you a vast selection for your deck. Combine two or more colors for a deck that's sure to attract attention. You can paint the decking and stair treads one color, the railings a second color, and the balusters a third. Unlike wood stains, paint will not change color according to the wood species: the color you buy at the store is the color your deck will be after it's painted, unless you apply a pale paint to a very dark wood. Be sure to buy a paint rated for outdoor use so that it can stand up to sun and rain as well as foot traffic.

① White
② Off-white
③ Brown mustard
④ Cherry red
⑤ Smoke gray
⑥ Golden harvest
⑦ Scarlet red
⑧ Burgundy
⑨ Bistre brown
⑩ Angora pink
⑪ Classic violet
⑫ Canyon blue
⑬ Dark fudge
⑭ Dark lilac
⑮ Grape
⑯ Harbor sky
⑰ Reddish brown
⑱ Smoky purple
⑲ Ultramarine blue
⑳ Periwinkle

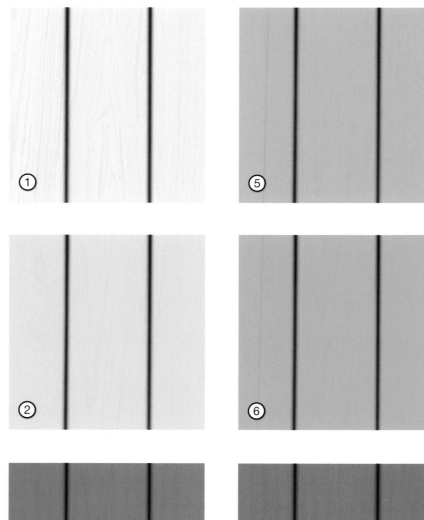

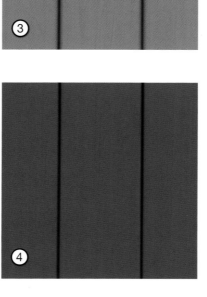

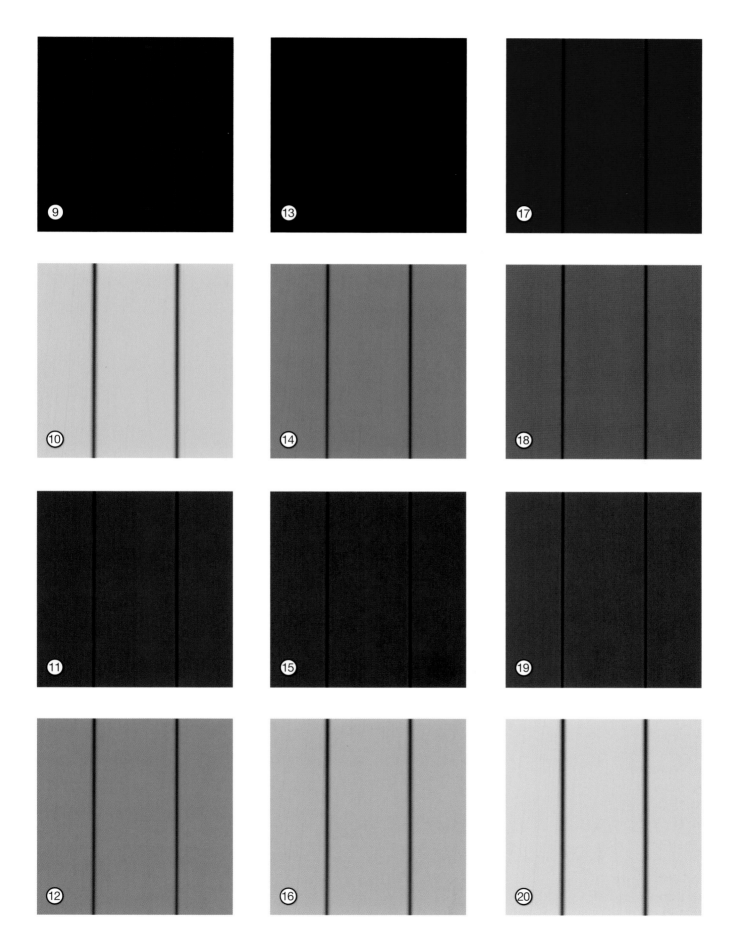

Continued from page 124.

Paint covers the wood grain and hides defects in the wood, making it a good choice for green-treated or lower-grade lumbers that don't look good in their natural state. This said, avoid paint for more expensive, attractive wood species like redwood or cedar. With these woods it is best to highlight the natural material rather than cover it. Paint offers excellent sun protection. The higher the gloss of the paint, the more shine it will have and the greater the sun protection. For new decks, apply a primer before painting.

① Misty blue
② Blue bows
③ Denim blue
④ Ink blue
⑤ Sky blue
⑥ Ocean blue
⑦ Sapphire
⑧ Midnight blue
⑨ Teal
⑩ Cool jade
⑪ Blue frost
⑫ Aqua green
⑬ Evergreen
⑭ Sea blue
⑮ Sea-lily green
⑯ Bell pepper
⑰ Turquoise
⑱ Ice blue
⑲ Green shimmer
⑳ Meadow green

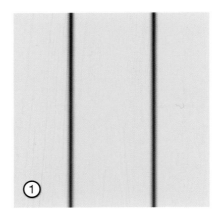

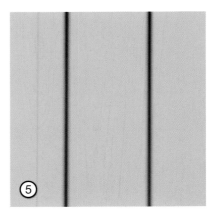

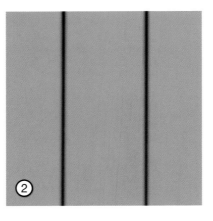

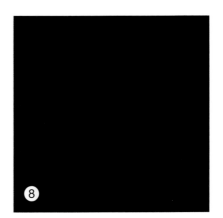

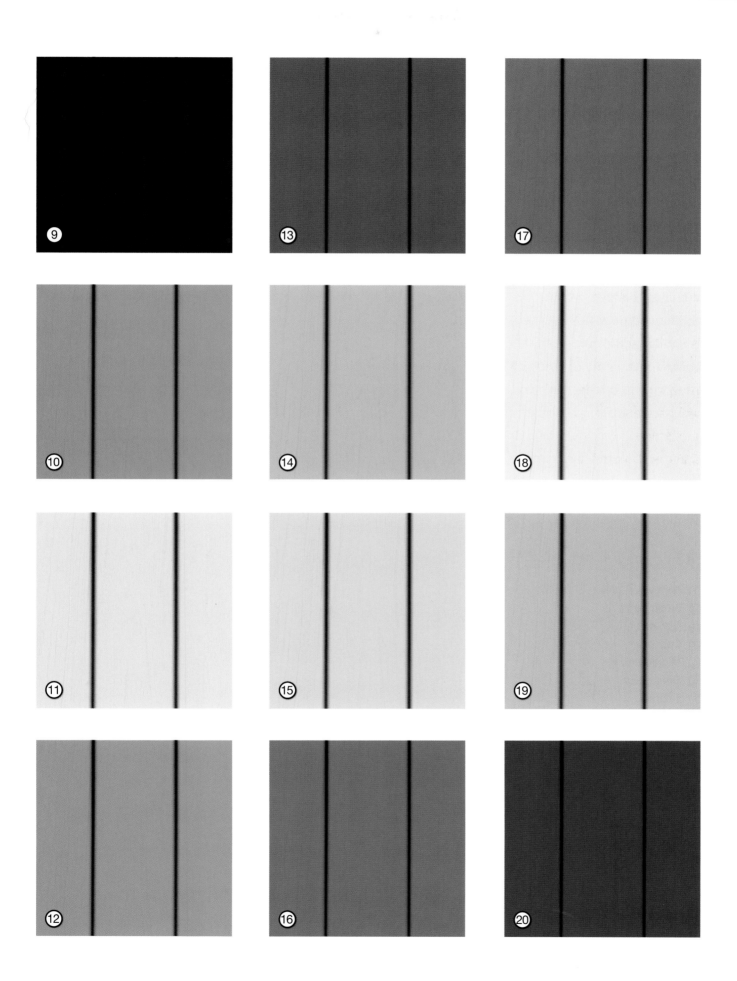

Continued from page 126.

Although a painted deck looks attractive, it requires regular maintenance. Since paint forms a film on the deck boards rather than penetrating the wood, like stains do, it will crack and peel as the wood expands and contracts with changes in temperature and humidity. Every few years, you'll need to scrape off the chipped and peeling paint, and apply a new coat. You won't have to strip the deck like you would with stain.

① Dark velvet green
② Bottle green
③ Fern green
④ Cool gray
⑤ Midnight forest
⑥ Olive green
⑦ Emerald
⑧ Warm gray
⑨ Charcoal
⑩ Burnt umber
⑪ Classic brown
⑫ Copper
⑬ Rust
⑭ Reddish brown
⑮ Warm brown
⑯ Straw
⑰ Rich caramel
⑱ Saddle brown
⑲ Raw umber
⑳ Pale gold

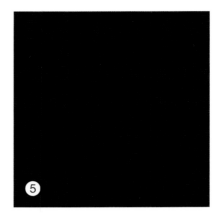

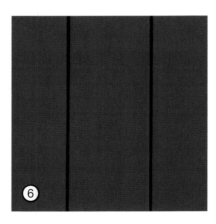

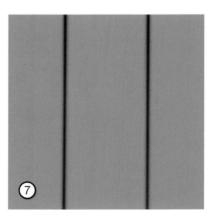

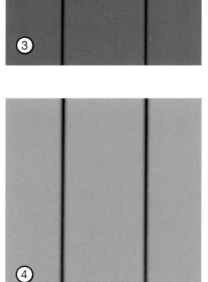

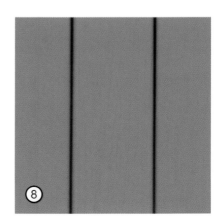

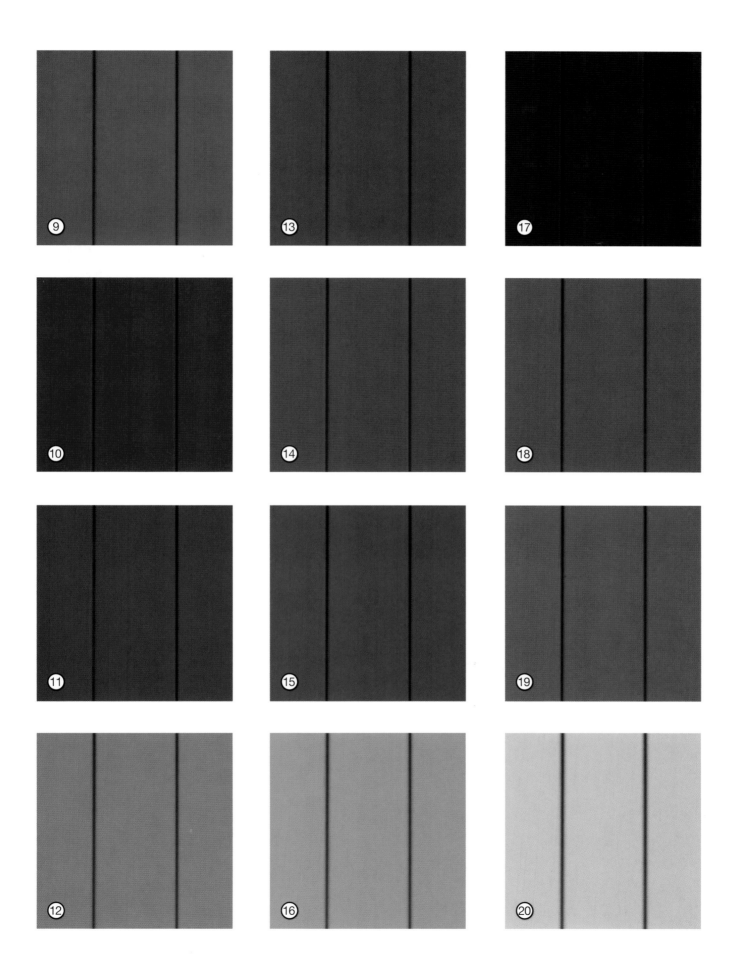

Paint and Stain

To accent certain components on the deck, use a combination of paint and stain. While most people would not want a brightly painted deck, strong colors provide a nice contrast to darker-stained wood when used conservatively.

Painting balusters or the entire railings a light color, such as white, and staining the rest of the deck a darker shade is a popular color scheme that brings decks to life. Another option is to paint accessories, like pergolas or trellises, and stain everything else.

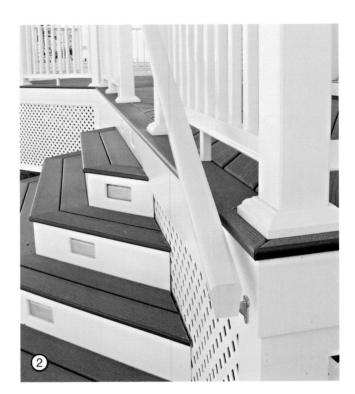

③

④

⑤

① Here, the posts, balusters, and railing trim are painted a light color, which matches the pergola. The decking, top railing, and planter boxes are stained darker for a good contrast.

② White railings, stair risers, a handrail, and lattice skirting look good against the brown-stained decking and stair treads on this deck.

③ Gray doesn't usually draw attention, but it does on these railings and posts. The paint complements the brown-stained decking, stairs, and skirting.

④ Light brown and bright white might not seem like a good color combination, but they work well together on this deck, partly due to the white siding on the house.

⑤ Gray composite decking and brown-stained planters blend together for a low-key, yet attractive deck.

Patio Materials

Patio materials set the style for your patio, giving it a high-end, sophisticated look or a playful, casual feel. Materials give the patio its color and texture. The surface is the first thing you and your guests will see every time you walk out onto the patio. The vast number of choices can seem overwhelming—everything from brick and stone to concrete, from pavers to tile, and from loose gravel to wood. Once you have chosen your materials, you still need to decide on a pattern. This chapter will help you decide what will work best for your particular patio.

Opposite: Subtle color variations in these gray, square pavers save this patio floor from bland uniformity. Joint lines are minimal.

Below: Masonry materials give patios a rustic charm as they age. The wooden chairs and table facing the tulip garden here fit in with the country theme.

Choose materials that will enhance your patio and its surroundings. Patio materials beside the house need to complement the house exterior. Masonry materials work in almost any environment, while tile and brightly colored concrete surfaces may prove distracting alongside colorful siding on the house. Be sure to use materials that suit your climate conditions. Areas that experience freeze and thaw cycles require non-porous materials that won't absorb water, freeze, and then crack.

Consider using two or more materials if 1) you can't narrow your favorites down to just one, 2) you have a lot of area to cover, or 3) you want to save money. For example, an elaborate stone patio near the house can give way to a less expensive concrete pathway or stepping stones. Similarly, brick can be combined with wood timbers to create a bold patio or a stepped walkway. You can also achieve your desired look by substituting less expensive materials that mimic the real thing. Pavers, brick, stone, and stamped concrete offer similar appearances to other materials, but at different prices and with different benefits.

The colors and prices of some materials, most notably brick and stone, often change by region. Geological variation will produce differences between brick manufactured locally and bricks produced in other parts of the country. The quarries closest to you will mine specific types of stone: not always the type you have in mind. If you're absolutely set on a specific material that's not readily available in your area, you can probably order it, but be prepared to pay extra.

Clay Brick

The distinctive look of brick and the myriad of bricklaying patterns to choose from make this humble material the most commonly used. It also works well with almost any house exterior and in any patio design.

Brick can be set over a sand base or held firmly in place with mortar. Either application produces an attractive, distinguished surface. Wide joints with visible mortar add a second color to the patio, while fitting the bricks tightly together eliminates the joints altogether, giving the patio a continuous look, uninterrupted by individual bricks. The drawback to brick is the cost; it is one of the most expensive patio materials.

① Brick is the obvious choice for this three-tiered patio because it complements the building's exterior and the steps. Stone edging adds the right degree of contrast.

② Bricks set in sand compose this patio, which is unassuming but large enough for a table and chairs. The patio is built into the ground so the bricks are level with the surrounding yard.

③ This pale-colored brick is laid in a running-bond pattern, creating a crisp look that blends seamlessly with the stucco siding and concrete patio beside the doors.

④ Here, pale-gray mortar in wide joints provides a contrasting color and emphasizes the darker bricks.

⑤ Set in a herringbone pattern with tight joints, the bricks used here have a sleek look that's perfect for a contemporary pool patio.

⑥ Common brick is arranged in a herringbone pattern here, which gives the patio a formal look. The impression is reinforced by an elegant patio set.

Bricks are available in a wide range of sizes, colors, and textures. The bricks most often used for patios and landscaping are "common" bricks, which have a rough texture, and "face" bricks, which have a smooth, almost slick surface.

Clay brick is an all-natural material, made by mixing clay with water then baking it in a kiln and cutting it to size. Different clays and additives used in the manufacturing process produce variation in colors and textures, resulting in hundreds of options.

① Burgundy brown
② Colonial red
③ Terra-cotta red
④ Red clay
⑤ Brown earth
⑥ Thundercloud gray
⑦ Cobblestone gray
⑧ Fossil gray
⑨ Rustic brown
⑩ Brownish red
⑪ Red sand
⑫ Warm brown

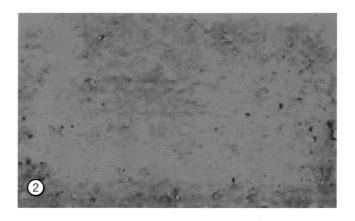

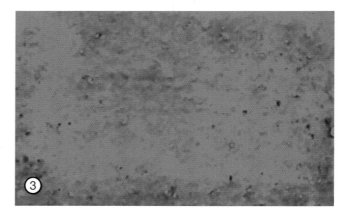

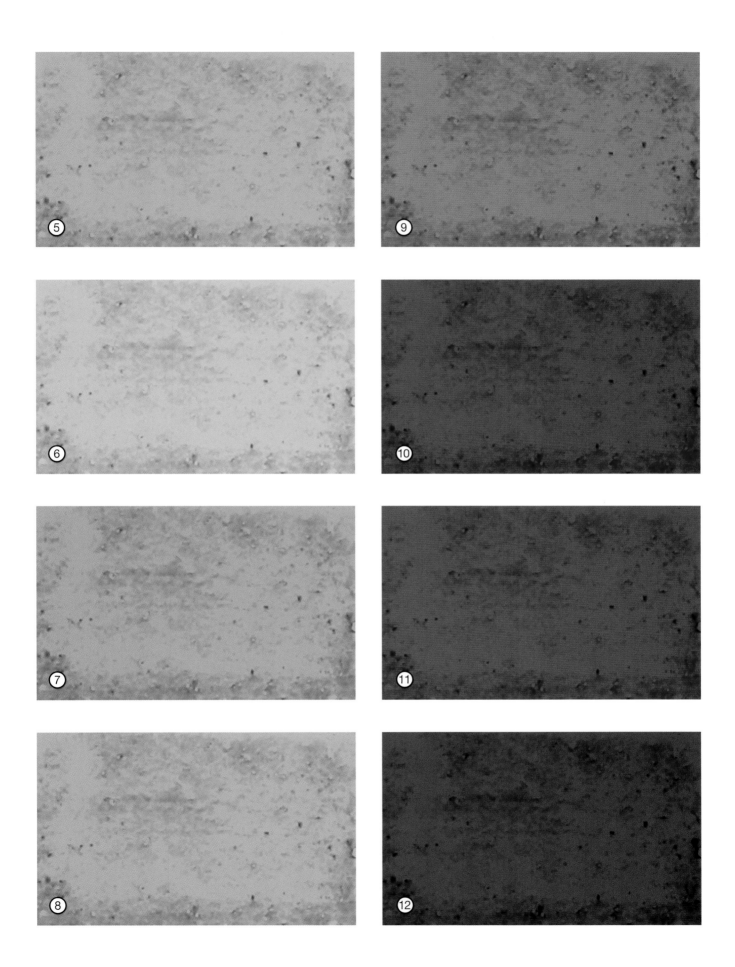

Stone has a natural beauty that gives patios a timeless look. A lot of shapes, colors, and surfaces are available, which often vary by region. Make sure the stone you choose is slip-resistant, especially if you're using it next to a pool. Stone is either cut into regular shapes, like square tiles, or in random shapes. Irregular-shaped stones look effective if they're arranged correctly, but the layout requires careful planning. Some designs minimize joints by placing the stones tightly together, while others leave large gaps on purpose, then fill them with mortar for a different look.

① Leaving large, mortarless gaps between these stones has left room for grass to fill in the joints.

② Various shapes and colors work together to give this patio a formal look. Keeping the joints tight maintains the focus on the patio as a whole rather than on individual stones.

③ Irregular flagstones are pieced together in a random pattern to create this attractive patio.

④ These pre-cut stone tiles have a uniform shape that gives the patio a linear appearance.

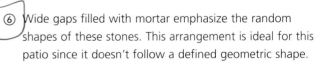

⑤ A smooth, level surface is important for this stone patio, as it provides comfort under bare feet. The stones are pre-cut in different shapes and sizes to add visual interest.

⑥ Wide gaps filled with mortar emphasize the random shapes of these stones. This arrangement is ideal for this patio since it doesn't follow a defined geometric shape.

⑦ Distinctly different stone shapes and patterns break this patio up into individual sections, which are tied together by the border around the pool.

Flagstone is a popular choice for patios. You can choose a texture that is comfortable without being slippery, and the appearance offers noticeable variation in color. Flagstone isn't actually a type of stone. Instead, it's a generic term for any large, flat stone that's split from limestone, sandstone, or slate.

Marble and granite are the toughest stones and less porous than sandstone and limestone. Make sure the stone you choose can withstand your climate conditions. Porous stones may absorb water, freeze, and then crack in cold temperatures.

① Golden garnet granite
② Silver, sea-green granite
③ Frosted antique-white limestone
④ Polished cream limestone
⑤ Brown granite with black streaks
⑥ Coffee-bean granite
⑦ Brushed, brown limestone
⑧ Brushed silver limestone
⑨ Streaked cream travertine
⑩ Natural white sandstone
⑪ Fossil sandstone
⑫ Amazon-green slate
⑬ Coral travertine
⑭ Natural brown sandstone
⑮ Sandstone with true fossil
⑯ Ivory slate
⑰ Sunset honed, unfilled travertine
⑱ Natural gray sandstone
⑲ Red sandstone
⑳ Rustic multicolor slate

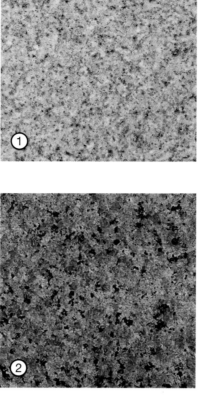

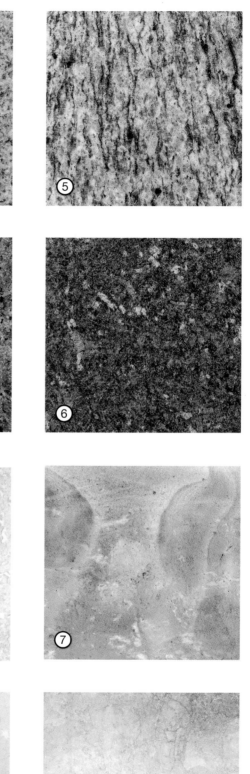

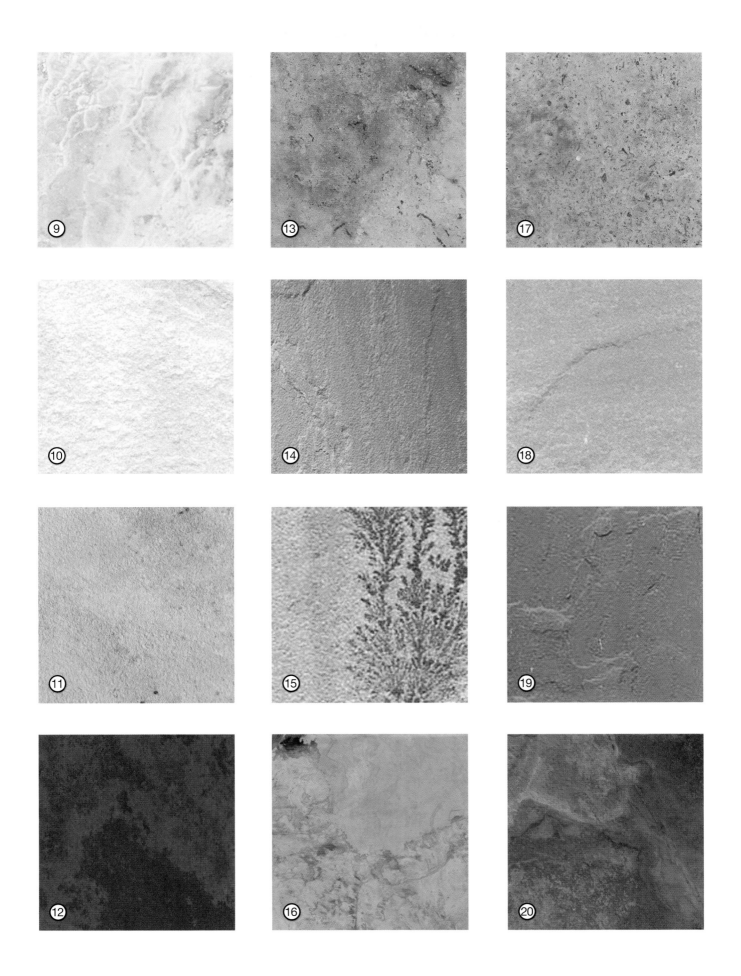

Concrete

Concrete offers more than just a bland slab outside a patio door. There is a range of colors, textures, designs, and patterns available. In fact, some stamped concrete looks identical to brick or stone, but doesn't have the high price. Seeded aggregates in concrete give it color and texture. Since concrete can fit any shape when poured, it's a good choice for patios or walkways with curves or rounded edges, which would otherwise require cutting of the material. Concrete patios typically have symmetrical lines running across the surface to control cracking.

① The seeded aggregate concrete surface here adds both texture and speckled colors to the patio, giving it a warm, inviting feel.

② This concrete patio matches the lightly colored stucco on the building, erasing the distinction between the outdoor living space and the house. The patio also provides a stark contrast to the green lawn, clearly defining the patio area.

③ The strong horizontals of the blinds and the vertical lines of the window frame complement the linear theme of the patio.

④ Concrete can fit almost any style and design, such as this contemporary patio. The straight, narrow lines in the concrete diverge nicely from the curves in the furniture.

Pavers

Pavers are available in many shapes and sizes. They can be butted together or interlocked like puzzle pieces to form intricate patio surfaces. Pavers are easy to install, making them the perfect choice for DIYers. They are placed over a compact bed of sand, then sand is swept into the joints. Although pavers are not difficult to work with, they often yield designs that look complex. They also work well as stepping stones, especially if they have an interesting shape or are embedded in loose materials such as gravel or river rock. Made of dense concrete, pavers are extremely tough and hold up well under traffic.

① Rectangular pavers with slightly different hues blend together to give this patio charm. The joints around the pavers are filled, but the lines are not a distraction.

② The brick pavers here mesh well with the brown deck and the paler brick on the house exterior.

③ It's nearly impossible to distinguish between pavers like these and actual stone. The soft colors in the pavers match the patio chairs.

④ Pavers offer color-blends that are not always available in natural stone. These pavers have an aged look, even though the patio is not very old.

⑤ Located next to a lake, this patio provides an ideal setting for overlooking the water. The pavers ensure that the surface is maintenance-free and are tough enough to handle constant foot traffic.

⑥ These pavers have light hues that give the patio a muted look. The pattern of large squares with smaller insets is simple, yet visually pleasing.

Pavers are widely available as squares, rectangles, circles, octagons, and other geometric shapes. They are designed either as regular pavers, which have flat sides that butt against adjoining pavers, or as interlocking pavers, with specially shaped sides.

Pavers can easily create complicated designs in the patio surface or pathways, or they can be arranged to form exciting patterns—like the popular circular designs. Besides being slightly less expensive than the brick or stones they replicate, pavers are available in an ever-expanding range of shapes.

① Brown brick
② Rustic brown brick
③ Reddish-brown brick
④ Faded brown brick
⑤ Cobblestone
⑥ Red stone
⑦ Grey stone
⑧ Interlocking concrete
⑨ Clay brick
⑩ Aged brick
⑪ Interlocking tan concrete
⑫ Interlocking custom concrete

①

②

③

④

Tiles

Tile is often used in kitchens and bathrooms, but can also be used outdoors as an attractive patio surface, either as the main material or as an accent. If you have tile indoors, using it in the patio is a great way to blur the transition from indoors to outdoors.

Unglazed tiles work best for paving because they offer some traction for walking. Glazed tiles, which often have brightly colored surfaces, are usually too slick to walk on, so use them as accents or edgings.

① The earth tones in the tile are a natural fit for this southwest-style setting. The tiles are placed at an angle so the grout lines intersect with the exterior walls.

② Completely surrounding the water fountain, square tiles are laid horizontally along the sides and diagonally along the top for a striking visual effect. Borders along the top emphasize the diagonal pattern.

③ These large, rectangular tiles are lined up to let parallel grout lines run vertically and horizontally across the patio.

④ Subtly different colors harmonize together in this tiled patio, giving the surface an attractive mix of soft colors that offer a pleasing contrast against the single color on the house's exterior.

⑤ Perfectly square tiles give symmetry to the floor of this outdoor room. The round furniture contrasts nicely with the straight lines in the patio.

⑥ Terra-cotta tiles with generous grout lines give this patio a modestly textured surface that will be comfortable to walk on—even with bare feet.

⑦ Tiles with a terra-cotta hue form a distinct border around this patio. Speckled gray tiles cover the patio surface, the sides, and the stairs.

Ceramic tile is one of the oldest known building products—and it's still as popular as ever. Made by mixing clay, sand, and other natural materials, which are then fired at extremely high temperatures, ceramic tile ranges from single, colored square tiles to decorative mosaics. Terra-cotta tile, with its familiar warm red color, and quarry tile, which is actually made from fired clay and comes in pastel colors, both fall into the category of ceramic tile.

① Frosted white
② Caribbean slate
③ Flagstone
④ Light mocha
⑤ Marbled white
⑥ Tuscan bone
⑦ Golden beige
⑧ Washed gray
⑨ Sahara beige
⑩ Washed brown
⑪ Faded beige
⑫ Slate
⑬ Brownstone
⑭ White sand
⑮ Muted copper
⑯ Aegean blue
⑰ Iris black
⑱ Bay sage
⑲ Acid-etched blue
⑳ Rusted brown

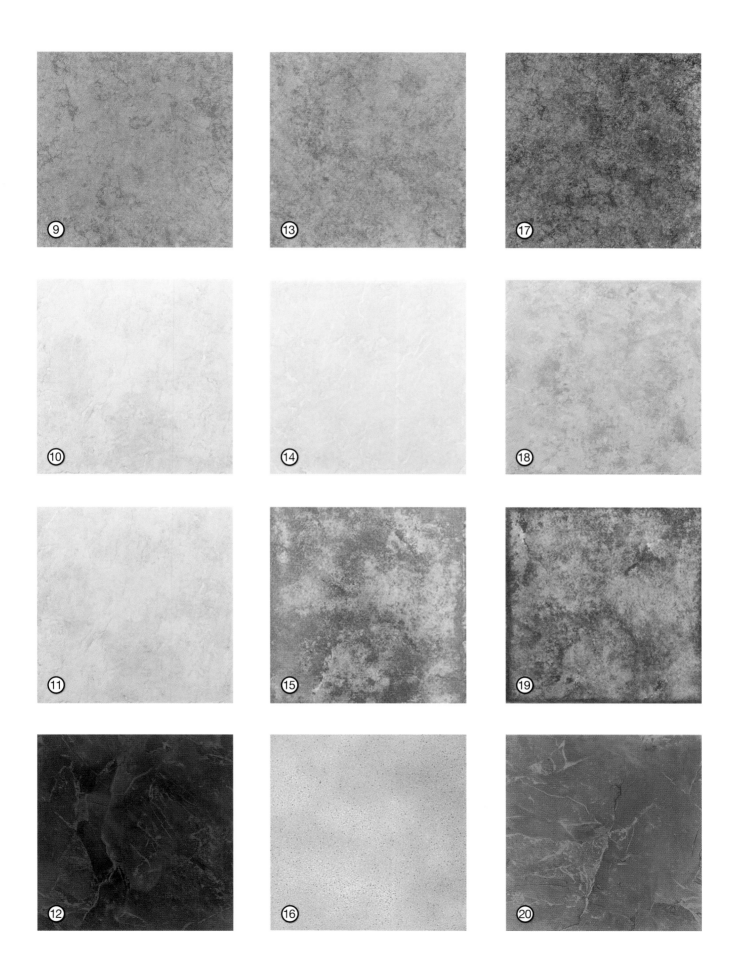

Porcelain tiles can look almost identical to slate, limestone, and other types of stone. They are also available in pastel colors. Standard 12-inch square tiles are the most common, though you can find them as large as 24 inches square or as small as 4 by 6 inches.

Porcelain tiles are very durable and easy to maintain—they're nearly stain-proof. Since they're impervious to water, they can be used in cold climates with freezing temperatures.

① Sandstone brown
② Slate
③ Etched black
④ Bluish gray
⑤ Royal gold blend
⑥ Mat brown
⑦ Storm-cloud white
⑧ Granite
⑨ Cream
⑩ Gray stone
⑪ Emperor dark
⑫ Washed brown
⑬ Light tan
⑭ Sand
⑮ Icecap white
⑯ Smoked gray
⑰ Dirty white
⑱ Charcoal
⑲ Red gold
⑳ Seasoned gray

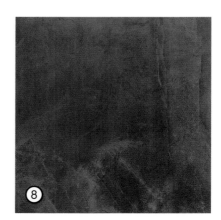
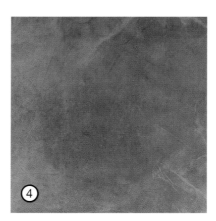
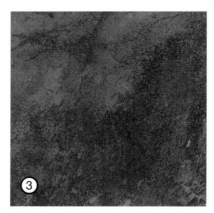
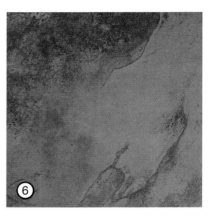

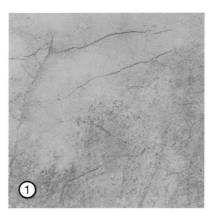
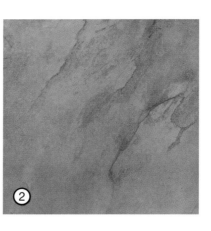
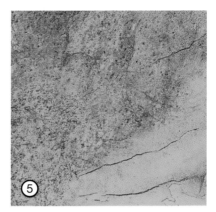

Adobe

Adobe bricks, blocks, and pavers are common materials in the southwest United States. Adobe materials used to be made by mixing clay and straw, cutting the mix into bricks or slabs, and then letting them dry in the sun. The materials could only be used in warm, dry climates, like the southwest. Adobe manufacturing has changed, so the materials can now withstand cold weather and can be used in any geographic region. Adobe materials are usually 4 inches thick and either butted together with no mortar between the joints or kept far enough apart to let grass or flowers grow in the gaps.

(5)

(4)

(6)

① Extremely narrow pavers are used on this patio every few rows to break up the rhythm and keep the joints from aligning. The result is a series of short, straight lines and long circular lines.

② Starting with a single, round piece in the middle, these pavers form an ever-widening circle that results in a perfectly round patio.

③ Several colors of paver blend together to give this patio its earthy look. The pavers are butted tightly together to form graceful curves.

④ Neutral-colored bricks with faint joint-lines direct the eye to this large, shapely pool.

⑤ Three sizes and two colors of paver lend an eccentric look and feel to this pathway as it winds down the hill between the concrete borders.

⑥ Adobe bricks are able to fit almost any design and color scheme. These bricks go together with the white steps and all three sidings on the house—not an easy task.

Adobe materials are traditionally a warm, reddish brown with an earthy look. The addition of cement products to the manufacturing process, which stabilizes the bricks or blocks, can give the bricks or blocks different looks. Adobe blocks are typically very large—up to 8 x 16 inches which makes them quite heavy to work with. It also allows a single block to cover a large amount of patio space. For that reason, large blocks are best suited to large patios where they're in proportion to their surroundings. Smaller bricks and pavers work well on any patio or walkway.

① Traditional red adobe brick
② Gray circular pavers
③ Gray bricks in a herringbone pattern
④ Red pavers in a curving pattern
⑤ Gray blocks in various sizes
⑥ Red-gray bricks in a random pattern
⑦ Irregular pattern with a mottled effect
⑧ Traditional red-gray adobe pavers
⑨ Gray and red pavers in a round pattern
⑩ Pavers in a circle design
⑪ Two brick shapes in red-gray
⑫ Multi-shaped pavers

Loose Materials

Hard, permanent surfaces such as brick and concrete aren't always the best choice for outdoor spaces. Areas around plants need drainage and flexibility to allow foliage to grow, and areas around children's play structures should be soft enough to cushion any falls.

Loose materials work well in such situations, and they can look nice in other applications, too. Stones, colored gravel, and wood chips add color and texture to patios. They're also the most inexpensive materials—useful when you're covering large areas. Be sure you have adequate edging to keep the materials from spreading all over the yard.

① White pebbles are a great match with these concrete retaining walls. Brightly colored pillows and blankets over the textured surface add a welcome dose of color.

② Sand keeps the mood light and casual on this back-yard patio. Raised edgings along the sides contain the sand.

③ Loose gravel is the perfect choice here. The light-colored surface balances against the darker walls, plants, and fence.

④ Combining loose materials with a solid surface is a great way to add flavor to a patio, as shown here. The upper level is built with stone, while the lower section is gravel with stone edging.

⑤ Solid pavers hold the table steady in the middle of this patio, while the rest of the surface is covered with loose materials.

⑥ Here, pea gravel makes the patio seem almost like a beach. The chairs sink into the gravel so they won't skid across the patio.

Loose materials come in several types, which are sold by the bag, ton, or cubic yard. You'll probably have to add new materials every couple of years as the surface compacts or the materials get displaced. Loose materials are typically laid 2 to 4 inches deep. Besides making excellent patio and garden cover, they also make great pathways and transitional spaces between areas of your yard.

① Wood mulch
② Shredded bark
③ Decomposed granite
④ Volcanic rock
⑤ Colored gravel
⑥ Quartz rock
⑦ River rocks
⑧ Pebbles
⑨ Sand
⑩ Blue crushed glass
⑪ Shredded wood
⑫ Wood chips

Wood

It may not seem a likely choice for patios, since it is usually confined to decks, but wood can make a superb patio surface, too; especially when installed in dramatic parquet patterns. Wood can be laid lengthwise, as it is on decks, or as interlocking wood tiles over concrete. Another popular application is placing wood timbers over sand. Short sections of timbers laid in a crisscrossing pattern give the surface added appeal.

① Interlocking wood tiles give this patio surface the same stately appearance as a formal dining room. Baseboard on some of the masonry walls hides the gaps between the floor and the wall.

② Timber sections painted in two different colors placed perpendicular to each other give the patio a checkerboard surface.

③ Reducers are placed along the edge of these wood tiles to graduate the step down from the wood patio to the slightly lower gravel.

④ Parquet gives this patio surface a unique look and design that can't be replicated by any other materials, and makes the confined patio appear larger.

⑤ The use of two contrasting shades of gray on this wood patio adds interest, without overwhelming the patio's overall color scheme.

⑥ Grooved wood planks help to make this balcony patio look like an actual bedroom. This type of wood feels comfortable underfoot, even when wearing slippers.

⑦ Wood planks cover this patio, giving it a country feel. Brick edging is a nice touch along the sides.

Combining Materials

With so many enticing patio materials to choose from, it's often difficult to pick only one. Fortunately, you don't have to. Combining two or more materials creates interesting patterns and contrasting colors that aren't possible when using a single material. Integrating materials requires a bit of extra planning to achieve the look you want. Patterns that feature a second material placed at regular intervals need to have precise spacing, since any inconsistencies will be very noticeable. Materials with different thicknesses need a specially prepared base to make the patio surface level.

① Here, making the transition from the patio to the deck requires abutting the stone surface to the wood decking.

② Wood planks, stone paving, and loose gravel, along with various edging materials, create an assorted mix as this walkway gives way to the patio.

③ Including gravel trenches in the concrete, as seen here, softens the shift from the hard concrete next to the house to the loose gravel in the yard.

④ Placing stones and flower mosaics in an uneven pattern gives this intimate patio a truly personalized look.

⑤ Great pains are taken to keep grass out of most patios, but it's welcomed here to enhance the design and to tie the patio into the nearby foliage.

⑥ At least four materials work together to create this visually stunning surface, which makes the space seem much larger.

⑦ Concrete and loose gravel form a checkerboard pattern on this back yard patio.

Accessories

Just as fashion accessories make an outfit, deck and patio accessories make an outdoor space: they increase comfort, functionality, and aesthetics for the life of the deck and patio. Think of your outdoor space as a constantly evolving work in progress. You can install new accessories to make the deck and patio more usable, modify the space to better suit your needs, or add finishing touches for a customized look. Bringing accessories onto your deck and patio allows you to personalize your outdoor space, often without spending a lot of money or making structural changes.

Plan your accessories around personal interests and activities. Young children will appreciate a play area complete with a sandbox; the family chef will like an outdoor cooking area with a patio cart on hand; and gardeners will enjoy maintaining flowerpots and planters. Interests change over time and accessories can change along with them. Turn play areas into water gardens or install a whirlpool to soothe tense muscles at the end of a busy day.

Accessories are a cost-effective way to liven up your outdoor space. For less than a hundred dollars, you can add portable lights to use the outdoor space after dark, install flower boxes to bring colorful plants onto your deck and patio, or erect a unique focal point—a sculpture, for example—to add interest. Easy-to-build firepits provide a gathering spot for family and friends. Or, if you want to think big, construct an overhead structure to block the elements. A patio heater will allow you to sit outdoors even in chilly weather.

Think about which accessories you want to add and where they'll be placed. Temporary accessories—such as portable canopies, umbrellas, tables, and chairs—can be conveniently taken down or moved, so they're only on the deck and patio when you want them to be. Permanent accessories often serve a dual purpose: they liven up the outdoor space by offering a "finished" look and they provide a specific use. For example, built-in benches are for sitting, gas grills are for cooking, and bridges are for crossing water ponds or streams.

Opposite: A table and chairs welcome guests onto this patio, providing a comfortable place to sit, converse, and enjoy the soothing sight and sound of running water.

Below: A stained-glass lantern provides a subtle decoration during the day, and illuminates the pathway after dark.

Outdoor Kitchens

When you're dining and entertaining outdoors, you don't want to have to run inside every time you need something. Outdoor kitchens put the cooking essentials right where you need them—in your outdoor space.

Modular kitchen units can be placed on patios, or you can have separate elements permanently built into the space. Commonly used kitchen items include a cooking surface, a refrigerator, and a sink. To upgrade an existing kitchen, add a wet bar, wine storage, cabinet storage, or food preparation area.

① Everything you need for outdoor entertainment is available in this compact cocktail unit. Stainless-steel appliances provide refrigeration and ice, and running water is available over the sink.

② A gas-grill kitchen is convenient for cooking on a patio. This kitchen unit is located far enough away from the seating area to allow smoke to dissipate.

③ A ceiling fan circulates air, shades block wind and sun, and an overhead structure keeps the rain out. You can enjoy a meal on this patio in any type of weather.

④ This modular kitchen consists of a grill, a refrigerator, and a cabinet on one side, and a bar for eating and drinking on the other side.

⑤ This full kitchen—complete with running water, a grill, an oven, a sink, and a refrigerator—is built into a brick setting, which matches the border around the stone patio.

⑥ This outdoor kitchen has a stove, a fridge, and an overhead rail with hooks for your utensils. Planters help to blend the kitchen into the outdoors.

Grills and Brick Ovens

Fully equipped outdoor kitchens are wonderful, but sometimes a simple grill is all you need. In fact, it's hard to picture a deck or patio without one. Cooking outdoors on a charcoal or gas barbecue is a summertime tradition and gives food an extra special taste, even if you end up eating it inside. Brick ovens are also growing in popularity. They look good, adding appeal to the patio, and are great for cooking the perfect pizza. Another plus is that brick ovens can be surprisingly inexpensive.

① Set on wheels for easy mobility, charcoal grills like this give food a smoky, campfire flavor.

② A basic gas grill cooks meals outdoors, which can then be served up on an outdoor table. If you have an incredible view like this, you'll want to spend as much time outside as possible.

③ Outdoor kitchens don't have to be large to be effective. This small oven gets hot enough to cook meals with an open flame.

④ Blending into the brick wall along the back of the patio, this brick barbecue cooks food over an open flame.

⑤ A standard grill like this is a staple on decks and patios. A heat mat underneath keeps spills from staining the patio surface.

⑥ Built into the corner of the patio, this brick oven is just the thing for cooking pizzas. The bricks are specially designed to handle extreme temperatures.

⑦ This modern gas grill is set in a concrete base that's built into the patio. Countertops are installed on both sides of the grill for holding food and condiments.

Dining Terraces

Dining terraces are dedicated areas for outdoor eating. The dining space is defined by nearby walls or railings, overhead canopies, or outdoor rugs as well as a dining table, chairs, and sometimes serving carts. Such details provide formal elegance.

Decide how much space you want for your dining terrace and whether it should be enclosed. Tables that seat six or more people require a fair amount of room—more than will fit under an umbrella or standard canopy.

① Formal dining settings are usually relegated to the dining room, but this one looks perfectly situated in a stately outdoor setting. Majestic columns mark the perimeter of the dining space.

② A round, compact table fits nicely in this courtyard, providing enough room for four people to sit comfortably.

③ Placing dining seating along the edge of a patio allows guests to sit in the shade while taking in the scenery.

④ A simple table and a few chairs are all that's needed to create a dining terrace on this back-yard patio.

⑤ This deck's lower level provides the perfect spot for a dining terrace. The table's rectangular shape mimics the shape of the rectangular deck.

⑥ There isn't much extra space on this patio tier, but it makes a cozy dining terrace that utilizes every inch.

⑦ Keeping the dining area next to the house, under the protection of a retractable awning, simplifies the task of bringing food and drinks from the indoor kitchen to the outdoor table.

⑧ Setting up a portable canopy over the table and chairs provides shade for the entire dining area, so it can be used throughout the day.

Tables and Chairs

If you want a place to eat dinner outside, unwind with a drink, or enjoy a conversation with friends, a table and chairs are a must. Table-and-chair sets are the accessories used most often, making them good investments. Furniture that's water-resistant, fade-resistant, and maintenance-free can be left outside without worry, while more valuable items are best protected by an overhead structure.

① A convenient basin in the middle of this table ensures that ice and cold drinks are always within arm's reach.

② This deck mimics the typical décor of an indoor sitting room, with matching chairs, end table, ottoman, and coffee table.

③ Despite being black, these transparent chair backings won't absorb heat, so they're comfortable for sitting even on sunny days.

④ Inexpensive and comfortable, this type of sling table-and-chair set is very popular for decks and patios.

⑤ Outdoor furniture can be both attractive and functional, as these handsome chairs demonstrate. A carpet outlines the sitting area.

⑥ Removable chair cushions add comfort to these hard chair seats and throw a dash of color across the monotone table and chairs.

⑦ Open to the weather and vulnerable to splashing in this poolside setting, the table-and-chair set and recliners here are made of low-maintenance metal and plastic.

⑧ This classical patio set fits in well outside an Old World house. The graceful curves on the table and chair arms follow the lines of curving walls and stairs.

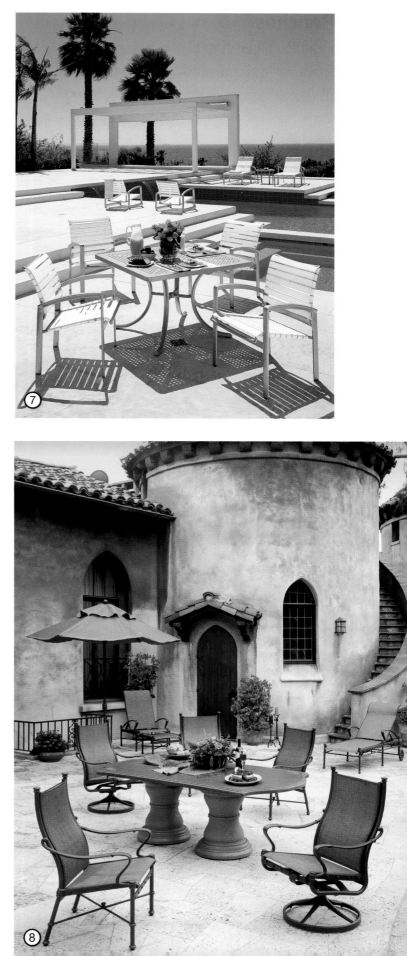

Benches

Including a bench or two in your outdoor space will guarantee that you always have a place to sit down. Build the benches with the same material as the decking so they look like a natural extension of the deck rather than a separate piece of furniture. Built-in benches along the edge of a deck will eliminate the need for railings, while a wooden bench along a walkway or pathway adds charm to the landscape. If possible, you may decide to convert the area under the seats into storage.

① These benches offer maximum seating in minimum space. Made of concrete, they complement both the brick wall and the gravel patio surface.

② Mimicking the circular pattern of the stone patio surface, this round table and bench are ideally situated in the center of the patio.

③ Although these slatted benches don't exactly follow the unusual curves of the deck, their rounded shape harmonizes with the winding railings.

④ This self-contained bench has everything you need: cushioned seats and backs, comfortable armrests, overhead shade, and portability.

⑤ Built-in benches make great additions to decks. These benches match the decking and use the railings as backing.

⑥ A lightweight yet sturdy bench, like this one, will fit almost any patio style and it is easy to move if you want to seek shelter from the sun or wind.

⑦ This yard was designed with a family in mind, starting with a long bench on the patio.

Other Furniture

Chairs, tables, and benches are the most common pieces of furniture on decks and patios, but they certainly don't have a monopoly on outdoor furnishings. Other types of furniture that make outdoor spaces even more enjoyable include: hammocks, daybeds, swings, rockers, heaters, and fans. A hammock is well suited for catching a catnap, while an outdoor bed lets you spend the entire night on the deck or patio. Don't overlook an old-fashioned swing seat, which can provide a romantic setting.

① A canopy bed offers outdoor sleeping on this rooftop patio. The bed is built into the wall around the patio and is painted to match.

② Attached to the gazebo and deck posts, this hammock is the ultimate piece of furniture for enjoying a lazy afternoon. As the sun shifts, the hammock will end up in the shade.

③ Reclining deck chairs provide comfortable places to sit and soak up the sun.

④ This patio swing is attached to overhead pergola beams by a rope. The swing is kept away from the house, trees, and other obstacles so it can move freely.

⑤ Placing a portable heater on the deck or patio warms the immediate area, making it especially welcome on cool evenings. Heaters like this will often become gathering spots when you're entertaining.

⑥ Wicker is an ideal material for this occasional table and chairs set, as it is light-weight and decorative.

Chair Options

Comfort is critical when choosing chairs, and they should also complement other outdoor furniture, either in color or style. The chairs shown here are comfortable, widely available, and look good in any outdoor space.

① Canvas sun chair
② Dark blue wicker bench with planter
③ Cushioned chair without armrests
④ Cushioned chair with armrests
⑤ Wicker armchair
⑥ Child's wooden chair
⑦ Black wicker chair with cushion
⑧ Director's chair
⑨ Dark blue wicker chair
⑩ Wicker chair with footrest
⑪ Round wicker chair

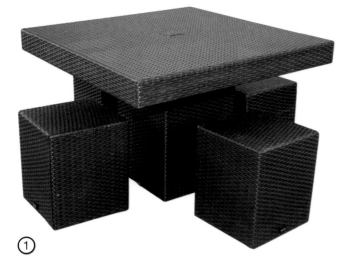

①

Dining Tables

A round table can seat several people without consuming a lot of space, but square and rectangular tables are more commonplace and match the design of most decks and patios. These pages show examples of attractive outdoor dining tables.

① Square wicker table with stools
② Wicker and metal table with benches
③ Rectangular wicker table with stools
④ Round wicker table with chairs
⑤ Wicker table with armchairs
⑥ S-shaped wicker table with chairs
⑦ Elevated rectangular table with raised stools

③

②

Lounging Furniture

You will need benches and reclining chairs for lounging and relaxing. Place cushion covers over the seats for increased comfort, and consider buying end tables to place nearby. Here are some ideas for stylish lounge furniture.

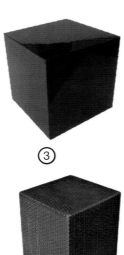

① Cushioned wicker sofa with coffee table
② Cushioned lounge chair
③ Brown lacquered end table
④ Black wicker stool
⑤ Black wicker cube
⑥ Wooden nesting tables
⑦ White wicker table
⑧ Cushioned sofa
⑨ Reclining vinyl lounge chair
⑩ Reclining wicker lounge chair with cushions

⑥

⑦

⑧

⑨

⑩

Hot Tubs and Whirlpools

Few deck features are as enticing as a hot tub or whirlpool. They're the ultimate outdoor luxury, providing a convenient retreat at the end of a stressful day, or serving as a romantic escape that's right outside the back door. The latest hot tubs and whirlpools are loaded with features, such as built-in televisions and stereos, for added enjoyment. It's best to include the hot tub or whirlpool when planning your deck or patio so you accommodate plumbing and electricity.

① Part of this swimming pool is reserved for a whirlpool, allowing users to relax in the warm water, then cool off with a swim.

② Built into the deck, this hot tub is secluded from the yard and neighbors. A solid fence further enhances the privacy.

③ This attractive hot tub has its own structure, containing a stepped patio surface, water running around the tub, and rocks on the periphery—all designed to enhance the hot-tub experience.

④ Space is restricted on this small deck, but there's still enough room for a striking stone structure to support a large whirlpool.

⑤ The merging of this spa tub with the swimming pool makes the tub look and feel much larger.

⑥ There's something for everyone on this dream patio: swimming, sunbathing, and relaxing.

Water Features

There is something hypnotic about water, which is why water features add such a tranquil quality to your outdoor space. The comforting look and sound of running or spraying water creates a serene, peaceful atmosphere. Water features are especially welcome in areas without lake or ocean views. And they don't have to be elaborate and expensive: a range of tabletop fountains plug directly into standard outlets. Of course, you can always think big and include a running-water garden, either built into the patio or raised above ground level.

① Gentle waterfalls at regular intervals turn an otherwise sedate strip into a lively pool with calming sounds.

② Everything you could hope for in a water feature is on display here: water gently cascades in tiers, sprays in jets between the pool and the garden, bubbles in fountains in the background, and falls from the second-story balcony.

③ This dolphin fountain adds a quirky detail to the edge of this pool.

④ It's difficult to not be enamored with a splashing waterfall. This one is surrounded by rocks and boulders for a natural look.

⑤ Not all water features need to be built into the ground. This self-contained system can be positioned on any solid surface.

⑥ A distinctive design—incorporating a wavy retaining wall and carved faces that spray water—makes this water feature one of a kind.

Water Gardens

Also known as aquatic gardens or garden ponds, water gardens combine a pool with water plants and sometimes goldfish, rocks, or fountains. Plants may be submerged completely, grow above the water with their roots submerged, or float on the surface. The toughest decision you'll have to make regarding water gardens is not whether or not to include one, but which one you want. Options are abundant, from quiet pools built into the ground to raised fountains surrounded by plants.

① A gentle waterfall prevents this water garden from becoming stagnant and offers the pleasant sound of running water.

② Rather than being in the water, broad-leafed plants in evenly spaced planters surround this still-water pool.

③ Built into the ground, this water garden is filled with plants, such as lilies, that turn the pool into a true garden.

④ This raised water garden curves stylishly along the front edge. Wide capstones can serve as makeshift seating—and make an ideal place for potted plants.

⑤ Rocks border this round water garden, and the shape is repeated in the curved line of the deck. The pool is shallow, but contains enough water to be effective.

⑥ Plants grow and float on the surface of the water in this contained garden, which is built on top of the patio surface. The elegant tiled sides add extra appeal.

Focal Points

Decks and patios can have a lot of elements competing for attention. To have a single item serve as a focal point, place it in a prominent location. The focal point doesn't have to be large and glaring; a simple statue or even a tree can work well. Anything that looks unique and draws the eye will make a great focal point, including items with a personal touch such as mosaic or hand-painted tiles.

① Falling water is certain to draw the eye, and the columned structure here makes it even more of a focal point.

② Planting a tree and then landscaping around it with colored gravel and large rocks have given this deck a dynamic point of interest.

③ The life-sized statue in the center of this shapely pool can be seen from anywhere on the patio.

④ Chairs face this magnificent stone fireplace just as they would in an indoor room, allowing people to sit back, relax, and watch the fire burn.

⑤ There's a lot to see from this patio, but the first thing people will notice is the eye-catching focal point near the water's edge.

⑥ This slender, leaf-shaped statue in the middle of symmetrical, manicured bushes is certain to catch people's interest and start conversations.

Planters

The easiest way to enjoy plants or trees in your outdoor space is to put them in planters. They're ideal for bringing greenery and colorful flowers onto wood decks and solid-surface patios. Planters can add style, set a theme, and define areas on a patio; they can be built into a deck; or they can be portable clay or ceramic pots that are easy to move around. Consider placing small planters on railings or benches to put them at eye level.

① The shiny planters here contrast nicely with the vivid green bushes. Stacking the planters together provides a wall of shrubbery.

② These planters have a decorative, upscale quality. Planters like this provide a range of layout options, and are easier to maintain than a full garden.

③ Sculptured shrubs and colorful flowers fill these oversized pots, which enrich the patio with plant life.

④ These shimmering planters bring a species of plant to the patio that would not normally grow in the region, while also enhancing the décor.

⑤ Simple plants that don't compete for attention are a natural fit for these contemporary planters.

⑥ These elegant planters can be easily transferred to anywhere on the patio, bringing much-needed color to the plain surface.

⑦ A single tree transforms the mood of this patio, thanks to a box-shaped planter.

Planters come in all shapes, sizes, and colors to hold anything from a single flower to a small tree. Be sure to place planters where you want before adding soil and plants, as they'll be too heavy to move once they're full. A selection of planters is featured here. Your local supplier will stock their own array of styles.

Flowerpots come in as many styles as flowers themselves! You can find flowerpots in almost any color and shape, making them an easy, inexpensive way to add excitement to your outdoor living area. Consider matching sets if you plan to feature flowers in several locations. Flowerpots are widely available in rustic terra-cotta, contemporary metallic, and sleek zinc-effect finishes, to name just a few. You will enjoy exploring the range at your local supplier, or even online.

Flower Boxes

If you want flowers raised up off the ground so you can enjoy them at eye level, add flower boxes. They are traditionally placed on deck or fence railings to house small, colorful flowers or creeping flowers that grow along the rails. They're also a lively addition to gazebos. If you don't have railings to support flower boxes, place them on half-walls or stairs, or hang the flowers in baskets from pergolas or other overhead structures.

① A flower box on this deck railing is right at home with the plants and trees growing all around the structure and in pots placed on the decking.

② Flower boxes overflowing with petunias line the top of these privacy deck walls. Matching planters built into the deck also welcome guests as they walk up the steps.

③ Hanging baskets of petunias are attached to the open rafter ends here, placing the attention-grabbing arrangements at eye level to people standing on the deck.

④ Pink pelargoniums spill over the railing and hide the flower boxes.

⑤ Flower baskets hang from these deck posts, while flower boxes on the decking are strategically centered between the posts for a balanced look.

⑥ Brightly painted portable flower boxes are butted together on top of these rails to display red pelargoniums with yellow and white annuals. The half-baskets fastened to the front of the railings contain the same annuals. Petunias are included in the top tier.

Trees

Trees block at least some sun and wind, increasing the comfort of the outdoor living area. They're also great for providing privacy, adding a colorful landscape, and housing birds and animals that you can watch when outside. Yet another benefit is being able to close your eyes and listen to a gentle breeze whistling through the branches. If you already have trees in your yard, plan your design around them. If not, plant new ones exactly where you want them. Choose trees that won't drip sap or drop seeds, and with roots that won't disturb your patio surface.

① This sprawling palm tree livens up the patio. The bushes growing at the base of the tree are also planted beside the house.

② A single tree is all that's needed to shade this entire patio, allowing people to eat at the picnic table while being protected from the sun.

③ The skirting around this tree matches the skirting around the whirlpool, tying the two elements together.

④ Tall and slender, this willowy tree provides a welcome contrast to the expansive, one-story house.

⑤ These tall, sculptured trees define the patio border and help screen the area behind it.

⑥ There's not much to this fledgling tree, but the special surface around it enhances its importance.

⑦ A dedicated planter near the pool allows this tree and the plants around it to flourish, bringing a touch of the tropics to the gray patio.

Arbors and Pergolas

Arbors are freestanding structures placed in an outdoor space, while pergolas are traditionally attached to the deck, patio, or house. Placing these structures over a deck or patio gives a sense of height. Even a small arbor or pergola with just a few rafters will draw the eye upward and make the space appear larger.

Cut the rafter ends in interesting shapes to give the structure extra appeal. Brightly painted or stained wood also commands attention. The rafters are very conducive to hanging flower baskets.

① This pergola incorporates both decorative and practical elements: a built-in bench for extra seating and overhead slats that support hanging baskets.

② This is a classic pergola style. Once again, a bench and flowerpots finish it off.

③ The angled cross-beams at the corner of this pergola match the angled design of the deck's upper level.

④ Plants have crept right up this post and across the underside of the arbor, filling the overhead area with flowers and shading the outdoor eating area.

⑤ This sturdy, four-cornered pergola makes an imposing presence on the deck. A slatted, angled design on top boosts the appeal.

⑥ Both sides of the pool are brought together by this bridging pergola. Benches are built into the structure on the left-hand side to form a convenient seating area.

⑦ Set at a slight angle and painted the same color as the railings, this pergola adds an additional feature to a bright and inviting deck.

Trellises

Trellises are decorative structures, consisting of horizontal, vertical, or diagonal parts, which are used to spruce up a deck or patio either by their own appealing design or by showcasing plants. Hanging baskets look great with trellises, as do climbing plants and flowers like wisteria or morning glories. Trellises are usually made out of wood or metal, but vinyl is becoming more common since it doesn't require maintenance. You will often find these structures filling in the sides of arbors and pergolas.

① Trellises wall off the sides of this deck behind built-in benches. The wood is painted white to match the pergola overhead.

② A wooden trellis takes the place of railings along the side of this deck. Climbing plants are beginning to grow over the slats.

③ Trellises are placed between the posts that support the simple pergola here. The trellises provide more privacy and more decoration than deck railings.

④ Roses entwine themselves through the holes in this lattice trellis, covering the surface with pink and green.

Overhead Structures

An overhead structure can define all or part of your outdoor living area by framing it from above. Design the structure to integrate with the house and the deck or patio. Putting a roof on the structure keeps the area underneath dry and shaded, making the space usable in unpleasant weather. If enclosing the area isn't important, a slatted or open roof is great for letting in natural light and allowing air to circulate. Adding an overhead structure to your outdoor space can be as simple as finishing the underside of a deck to protect a patio below it, or as creative as building an entirely new structure. Giving the structure a rounded or unusual shape enlivens the space, while supporting it with columns gives it a formal presence.

① Here, rafters support a climbing vine. The structure is kept open to let in the sunlight and fresh air.

② Columns support this entirely filled-in structure, which shades a patio dining area underneath.

③ This pergola has custom-cut ends that attach to both the house and the supporting beams.

④ The curved top of this overhead structure complements the round patio. The gigantic structure covers the entire patio surface, offering a retreat from the sun.

⑤ Intersecting geometric shapes give this structure an unusual yet appealing design.

⑥ Tightly spaced slats on this overhead structure cast a slotted pattern on the posts and patio surface, giving them a surreal appearance.

⑦ This rounded overhead structure mimics the shape of the rounded patio surface.

①

Gazebos

If you want an impressive outdoor structure you can use in rain or shine for entertaining friends or just sitting alone to read, you'll be hard-pressed to find a better environment than a gazebo. A gazebo might be physically attached to your deck or patio, or placed elsewhere in the yard and connected to your deck or patio via a pathway. Open on all sides with a solid roof, gazebos offer shade, basic shelter, a place to sit down, and open views. Whether they're colorful Victorian designs or maintenance-free vinyl constructions, gazebos quickly become favorite gathering spots for family and guests.

②

③

① This octagonal gazebo has metal rails, a beam ceiling, and a ceiling fan with lights.

② Attached to the back of the deck, this gazebo is painted a different color from the deck and has a different railing system. The result is that each structure has its own feel.

③ This gazebo is located close to the house, for ease of access. Food and drinks can easily be carried from the house to the sheltered outdoor dining area.

④ Screened-in sides keep pesky insects out of this gazebo. Double doors with screens also help to keep the gazebo mosquito-free.

⑤ The deck railing here blends seamlessly into the gazebo railing, making the gazebo seem like a natural extension of the deck.

⑥ This gazebo is connected to a raised deck. Both structures are built from the same wood for a unified look.

Bridges

Nothing captures the idea of open
outdoor space better than a bridge.
Bridges enhance the landscape,
bringing with them a feeling of
serenity. Having a pool or stream is
not a prerequisite for a bridge. Of
course, running water is certainly a
fitting setting, but placing the bridge
over a grassy ravine or connecting two
areas in the yard are other possibilities.
Complete the scene by including a
pathway or stepping stones to and
from the bridge.

① Made out of a giant stone slab, the bridge atop these stone stairs crosses a narrow section of the pool. It enables people to walk across the pool without having to walk all the way around it.

② This solid wood bridge connects deck stairs to the large, brightly lit gazebo. The bridge crosses a water garden, plants, and a stone wall.

③ A stepping-stone pathway leads to this short wooden bridge, which has a gentle slope as it crosses the plant-filled ditch.

④ Hidden behind trees at the end of the pathway, a classic-shaped residential bridge with railings is located in a picture-perfect setting.

⑤ This innovative stone bridge spans a meandering pool. The stone used for the bridge is different than the stone used for the patio to allow the crosswalk to really shine.

⑥ Arching between the wooden deck and the brick patio, this bridge offers a convenient way to cross the pool.

Shade Structures

Shade structures can partly or entirely block out the sun's rays on your outdoor space. Most shade systems are portable or mount to the house, so they're easy to set up or install after the deck or patio has been built. Propping up an umbrella over a table or a reclining chair is one of the most popular and inexpensive ways to get shade. Awnings are also common. Consider retractable models that fold out of the way when they're not needed. New models have remote-control options that allow you to open and retract the awning with the push of a button.

① You can't beat a simple umbrella for shading a small area, like the table and chair seating here. Adjust the umbrella to follow the sun.

② Umbrellas like this one come as part of a matching table set. They provide decoration as well as shade.

③ Nylon covers stretched tight between four corner posts provide shade for most of this deck. The overlapping triangle shapes give the structure added appeal.

④ This temporary structure can be set up anywhere in just a few minutes for instant shade.

⑤ This four-cornered canopy looks attractive and gives the patio setting a formal look. The fabric tied in the corners can also close to provide shade along the sides.

⑥ Retractable awnings extend over this outdoor space to provide shade, then pull back when not needed.

⑦ Besides blocking shade, awnings can also block light rain so you can enjoy the deck in various weather conditions.

⑧ Several awnings are attached to this building to keep the majority of the extensive patio shaded at all times.

⑨ It takes a special shade structure to complement this stucco house, and the red fabric gets the job done.

Kids' Play Areas

When designing your outdoor space, carve out a place for the kids. This gives them a dedicated place to play that's safe and specifically geared for their interests. Swing sets, play structures, and sandboxes are children's favorites, while a place to grow vegetables or flowers will promote an early interest in gardening. Choose a space that's at least partially shaded, and install a surface that's soft enough to cushion falls, such as pea gravel or sand. Make sure the play area is in a location that you can easily monitor, for peace of mind.

① A child-sized teepee is set up on this patio to give kids a fun place to play.

② The lower level of this deck is reserved for children. A brightly colored, plastic picnic table can be used for playing, coloring, and eating outside. A safety gate at the stair entrance keeps kids on the deck.

③ Play structures like this one are perfect for kids of all ages. The finished roof provides shade, while the rail-enclosed structure acts as a fort. Slides, a mounted telescope, and grab bars will hold kids' interest and keep them active.

④ This well-equipped play area will keep kids busy for hours. The giant sandbox ensures they won't get scraped or bruised if they fall.

⑤ Something as simple as a fun shape can allow kids to feel as though they have their own special space to interact with playmates.

Firepits and Fireplaces

There's something magical about sitting around a campfire with friends and family. Fireplaces and firepits bring that magic to your outdoor space. Besides providing warmth to the deck or patio on a cool evening, a fireplace serves as a central gathering place for relaxing and sharing stories. Built-in stone fireplaces have a commanding appearance, while portable firepits can be brought out for impromptu parties. Gas models are available, but the crackling sound and the smell of a real wood fire is perfect for the outdoors.

① Notice how the wood-burning fireplace is actually located just off the patio. This allows the smoke to dissipate freely without discoloring the overhead beams.

② Although the actual fireplace here is rather small, the structure is large and solid and the colors match the siding and trim on the house. The top of the fireplace makes a great shelf.

③ Dominating the end of the patio, this fireplace completes this cozy outdoor setting, which closely resembles an indoor living room.

④ The circular shape of this firepit encourages everyone to pull up a chair and feel the fire's glow.

⑤ The contrast between fire and water is aptly captured by this firepit—set into the patio surface beside the pool.

⑥ A nook in this specially designed wall is the perfect place for this wood fireplace. The mosaic on the chimney adds a classical touch.

⑦ This masonry firepit is built up on top of the patio and accommodates a small, comforting fire.

Built-in Lights

Lighting an outdoor space lets you enjoy your deck and patio whenever the mood strikes—even if it's during the middle of the night. The lights also increase safety by illuminating stairs, railings, and pathways. Built-in lights mean all you have to do is walk outside and flip a switch to instantly light up your space. Plan convenient switch locations and decide how much light you want and where you want it. A couple of low-wattage bulbs may be all you need to highlight a specific area of the deck or patio.

① These small lights don't grab attention, yet they're enough to highlight the stairs for safety.

② Built-in lights mark the edge of this pool and allow for after-dark swimming.

③ Lights built into the middle of each stair riser guide people safely up the stairs, around the pool, and toward the covered structure at the top.

④ Pairs of lights illuminate each side of this hot tub, while lights inside the tub make the water glow.

⑤ Flickering kerosene flames have a historic charm, and they effectively light up a pathway after dark.

⑥ Lights in the soffits brighten up this patio next to the house, while low-wattage bulbs mark the area around the pool.

⑦ A series of lights on the patio and in the water keep this area well lit.

Portable Lights

Portable lights can illuminate any outdoor space, including dark stairways, without requiring electricity. These lights can run on batteries or fuel, but are more often solar powered. They look just as stylish as lights powered by electricity, but they can be placed anywhere on your deck or patio without affecting your electric bill. Even if you already have electricity in your outdoor space, portable lights effectively illuminate areas where the power doesn't reach, such as along a pathway.

① These fixtures are filled with fuel, then the wick is lit. The burning flame throws off a natural glow that's reminiscent of old kerosene lamps.

② You can move this table set anywhere on the patio without worrying about awkward extension cords.

③ Small, flickering flames in each of these tall lamps illuminate the eating area on this elevated deck. The lamps match the metal deck rails and the table.

④ This solar light fixture, which resembles an old-fashioned street-lamp, lights the patio from behind a retaining wall.

Portable lights with an open flame have a magic that can't be duplicated with lightbulbs. From small candle holders to large fuel-burning fixtures, and even "candle gardens" in planters, these pages show some of the portable light styles available for your deck or patio.

Storage

You can never have enough outdoor storage space, so look for ways to include storage whenever possible. Storage areas are most effective when they're hidden: underneath a deck, for example, beneath a seat on built-in benches, or under stairs.

You'll want a place to store furniture cushions, garden hoses and tools, and table accents. A larger area, like under a deck, will provide enough space for long-handled garden tools and lawn equipment, such as mowers, so they won't clutter your garage.

1. The generous amount of space under this deck and stairs can store a lot of lawn and garden equipment.

2. Wood skirting planks installed at an angle give the underside of this deck an attractive, finished look and disguise the fact that it's a storage area. The double door allows for garden tractors and lawn mowers to be stored here easily.

3. A door under this stair landing provides access to a storage area big enough to hold the barbecue grill. The lattice skirt turns the storage space into an attractive feature.

4. There's not as much storage space under these bench seats, but every little bit helps. This space is big enough to hold garden hoses, which would look unsightly strewn across the patio.

5. Building a small structure like this provides a convenient place to store untidy items, like trash bins, where no one can see them.

Practical Checklist

1. BUILDING PERMITS

Building permit requirements change by jurisdiction. Decks almost always require a permit, but patios may not. Before starting the project:

- Check with your local building department to find out if a permit is needed and what restrictions, if any, you'll need to follow. Permits are usually required for decks, large structures such as gazebos, and projects involving plumbing, electrical work, and structural changes to the house.
- If your project requires a permit, have the blueprints, including detailed drawings and the type of materials and fasteners that will be used, reviewed by a building inspector. During the building process, have the project inspected as required.
- Find out any set-back restrictions on where you can place your structure or patio. Also find out any height restrictions on fences and walls.
- Have your property line marked if you plan to install a fence or wall along your property's border so you don't cross into your neighbor's yard.

2. CHOOSING MATERIALS

Different materials lend themselves to different applications, different environments, and result in different appearances. When you buy materials, consider these factors:

- Look at the materials in person before buying. Don't trust brochures or your computer to give you accurate colors.
- Buy an extra 10 to 15 percent of the materials needed to account for waste and scrap.
- If buying large quantities of lumber or masonry products, consider having them delivered rather than transporting them yourself. Ask about delivery fees and decide if the cost is worth it.
- Find out how the material should be stored before it's installed. Some products have specific storage requirements to keep the wood from warping.

3. BUDGETING

Decks and patios tend to be expensive, especially if they include luxury items such as pools, gazebos, or full-service kitchens. Before settling on a plan, consider these factors:

- Can you get the same look you want by using less expensive materials?
- Can you build the outdoor space in sections so you can spread out the cost over a longer time period?
- If hiring a professional to do the work, see if there's work you can carry out yourself to save money.
- Decide how much you want to spend on your project, then work with a professional to see what options are available for your money.

The table below will help you weigh up the look you want against what you can afford.

Material	Colors	Base required	Price
Brick	Reds, browns, tans, grays, white, earth tones	Gravel, sand, concrete	Expensive
Stone	Reds, light blues, cream, grays, browns, color variations	Gravel, sand, concrete	Moderate to expensive
Concrete	Dull gray, but can be colored	Gravel, sand	Inexpensive
Pavers	Reds, browns, grays, tans, earth tones	Gravel, sand, concrete	Moderate
Tile	Any color	Concrete	Moderate to very expensive

4. DIY OR PROFESSIONAL?

You'll need to decide if you can handle the design and building of your project yourself, or if you need to hire a professional. To help you choose between doing it yourself and hiring a professional, consider these factors:

- What are your specific skills? Can you make design decisions based on your existing knowledge?
- If the project is complex, involves structural changes to the house, or is beyond your level of expertise, hire a professional to ensure the project is done correctly.
- If the project requires running electric cable and making electrical connections, hire an electrician.
- Decide which portions of the project you can do yourself, then plan a building schedule to make best use of the professional's time.
- Decide if you can handle the physical requirements. A patio may require lifting heavy stones or installing a lot of brick. A deck may entail working on ladders to install beams and joists a story or more off the ground.
- Decide if you have the time. Building a deck or patio can take weeks, if not months, to complete.

5. CHOOSING A PROFESSIONAL

Different types of professionals are available to help with your project. Here are some of the professionals you can hire:

- General contractors specialize in building construction. Hire them for building decks.
- Landscape contractors specialize in lawn and garden construction. Hire them for building patios, gardens, or landscaping.
- Specialty contractors handle a specific area of construction, like concrete or electricity. Hire them for specialty work that requires specialty tools.
- Architects are licensed professionals with architectural degrees. They design structures that are sound and in accordance with building codes. Hire them for designing decks, gazebos, or patios.
- Landscape architects also have architectural degrees and specialize in designing lawn and garden projects. Hire them for designing retaining walls, gardens, and landscaping projects.
- Designers are not licensed like architects, but they usually have architectural training. They can design and build projects. Hire them for designing and then building decks, gazebos, and patios.
- Draftsmen produce working drawings or blueprints for structures that are needed to get a building permit. Hire them for drawing blueprints or plans for deck and patio projects.

6. HIRING PROFESSIONALS

When hiring a professional, whether it's a contractor, architect, or designer, follow these steps:

- Get recommendations from family and friends who have hired professionals. You can also find professionals in your area by contacting trade associations.
- Narrow your list of candidates to two or three. Meet with them in person and ask to see portfolios of their work and references. Call the references and ask questions about their experiences with the contractors.
- Have a clear understanding. Know what you want to accomplish with your outdoor spaces. Write down a clear list of goals. If possible, have photos from magazines or the internet of the type of deck or patio you want to have built.
- Keep in mind a realistic budget for how much you are prepared to spend.
- Before you make any payments to the professional and before any work starts, have a detailed contract signed by both you and your professional. The contract should cover what will be included in the project, the cost of the project, and approximate start and finish dates.

Glossary

Accent: Something used to draw attention to or highlight a particular feature or space on a deck or patio.

Accent lighting: Lighting that emphasizes a certain object or space.

Aggregate: Crushed rock used in patio surfaces.

Ambient lighting: The general lighting of an area.

Annual plant: A plant that completes its life cycle in one year.

Arbor: A freestanding structure that contains an overhead feature, usually placed at an entrance to a patio.

Backlighting: Lighting an object from behind or the side to create a silhouette.

Baluster: Vertical member that fits between the top and bottom rails in deck railings.

Base: Compact soil or gravel bed under a patio surface.

Beam: Structural member on a deck that's placed on top of the posts and supports the joists.

Biennial plant: Plant that lives for two growing seasons.

Building codes: Municipal regulations governing building practices and procedures.

Building permit: Certificate or stamp given by the building department after the building plans have been reviewed and approved.

Built-in: An object or accessory that is permanently attached to the deck or patio, or part of the main structure.

Canopy: An overhead structure or fabric that shades the area underneath it.

Cantilever: The end of a joist, or the end of an entire deck, that extends past the beam and is held in place by the weight of the structure behind it.

Cap: The top piece of a post.

Clearance: The amount of space between two pieces of material or around doors or furniture. Some clearances, such as the space between balusters, are governed by building codes.

Decking: The floorboards on a deck that are installed over the joists.

Drainage: The running off of water from the ground. Surface drainage occurs above the ground. Subsurface drainage occurs below the ground.

Edging: A line of material that visually separates one element from another, such as along a patio to separate the surface from the surrounding area.

Entry garden: A landscaped area near an entrance, for example the stairs on a deck, that draws attention to the entrance.

Face board: Wood used to cover the rim joists and end joists to give the deck a finished look.

Fascia: Horizontal trim piece that covers the exposed end of deck boards.

Firepit: A well used to contain a fire outdoors.

Focal point: A design element used to draw attention or dominate a space.

Footing: The concrete structure extending below the frost line that supports a deck post.

Grade: The top surface of the ground. "Above" grade means at or over ground level. "Below" grade means beneath ground level. ·

Ground cover: The name for plants that grow horizontally along the ground.

Hardscape: Sidewalks, patios, walkways, or other masonry products that cover the ground.

Inset: An area of the deck that's been cut out to make room for something else, like a tree or access to a light fixture.

Joist: A length of timber or steel, placed over the beams, that supports the deck structure.

Lattice: A crisscross pattern, usually thin, made out of wood, plastic, or metal.

Ledger: The piece of lumber attached to the house, which supports the joists on decks.

Low-voltage lighting: Outdoor light fixtures that are powered by low-voltage transformers.

Masonry: A generic term for stone, brick, and concrete products.

Mortar: A cement and sand product that is mixed with water to hold masonry products together in walls and patios.

Mortar joints: The gaps between masonry or tile materials that are filled with mortar.

Mulch: A layer of material, usually organic, that's placed around plants to keep in moisture and keep out weeds.

Open step: Stairs without risers between the treads.

Path lights: Lights placed along a pathway or walkway to illuminate the area. The lights are usually identical and held by stakes driven into the ground.

Perennial plant: A plant that lives more than two years.

Pergola: A framed structure built into the deck with overhead rafters.

Privacy fence: A solid fence that you cannot see through.

Proportion: How objects or parts of the deck or patio relate to something else, based on their size.

Raised bed: A garden bed that is higher than the surrounding area.

Retaining wall: A wall made of masonry or wood to hold back soil and provide level ground surfaces.

Riser: In stair construction, the piece of lumber placed between the stair treads. The vertical distance between the treads is called the rise.

Run: The length of a step.

Scale: The size of an object as it relates proportionally to nearby objects and its surroundings.

Set back: The required distance from a property line that a structure, such as a deck or gazebo, can be placed. Set backs are established by local municipalities.

Site plan: A hand drawing that includes the house and yard used to plan the location of a deck, patio, or landscaping.

Slope: A measure of the amount the ground surface rises or falls over a specific distance.

Softscape: The generic name for natural elements, like plants and trees, used in landscaping.

Spindle: A narrow, decorative baluster.

Stand-alone structure: A freestanding structure that is not built into or part of another structure.

Symmetry: Having both sides of an object, deck, or patio arranged identically.

Tread: The horizontal member on stairs that people step on when walking up the stairs.

Zoning requirements: Local ordinances that dictate where decks and patios can be located and their overall size and height.

Resource Guide

The following list of manufacturers, associations, and outlets is meant to be a general guide to additional industry and product-related sources. It is not intended as a complete listing of products and manufacturers represented in this book.

ASSOCIATIONS

American Fence Association
800 Roosevelt Road
Building C-312
Glen Ellyn, IL 60137
Tel: 800 822 4342
www.americanfenceassociation.com

American Society of Landscape Architects
636 Eye Street, NW
Washington, D.C. 20001
Tel: 202 898 2444
www.asla.org

Association of Pool and Spa Professionals (APSP)
2111 Eisenhower Avenue,
Alexandria, VA 22314
Tel: 703 838 0083
www.theapsp.org

California Redwood Association
405 Enfrente Drive
Suite 200
Novato, CA 94949
Tel: 888 225 7339
www.calredwood.org

The Engineered Wood Association
7011 South 19th
Tacoma, WA 98466
Tel: 253 565 6600
www.apawood.org

Hearth, Patio & Barbecue Association
1901 North Moore Street
Suite 600
Arlington, VA 22209
Tel: 703 522 0086
www.hpba.org

North American Deck and Railing Association
P.O. Box 829
Quakertown, PA 18951
Tel: 888 623 7248
www.nadra.org

Southern Pine Council
P.O. Box 641700
Kenner, LA 70064
Tel: 504 443 4464
www.southernpine.com

Western Red Cedar Lumber Association
P.O. Box 952
Riverhead, NY 11901
Tel: 800 266 1910
www.wrcla.org

Western Wood Products Association
522 Southwest 5th Avenue
Portland, OR 97204
Tel: 503 224 3930
www.wwpa.org

DECKING & MATERIALS

Artisan Quality Decks
1516 Willow Bead
Woodstock, GA 30188
Tel: 404 775 7942
www.artisanqualitydecks.com

CertainTeed
P.O. Box 860,
Valley Forge, PA 19482
Tel: 800 782 8777
www.certainteed.com

CorrectDeck
8 Morin Street
Biddeford, ME 04005
Tel: 877 332 5877
www.correctdeck.com

Decking For Less
21 Chivers Road
Chingford, London E4 9TD
England
Tel: +44 20 8926 8873
www.deckingforless.co.uk

DecKorators
50 Crestwood Executive Center
Suite 308
Crestwood, MO 63126
Tel: 800 332 5724
www.deckorators.com

Divine Construction
19118 Windsor Road
Triangle, VA 22172
Tel: 571 283 4607
www.divine-construction.com

Elyria Fence
230 Oberlin-Elyria Road
Elyria, OH 44035
Tel: 800 779 7581
www.elyriafence.com

Fiber Composites
34570 Random Drive
New London, NC 28127
Tel: 704 463 7120
www.fiberondecking.com

Fortress Iron
P.O. Box 831268
Richardson, TX 75083-1268
Tel: 866 323 4766
www.fortressiron.com

GeoDeck
1518 South Broadway
Green Bay, WI 54304
Tel: 877 804 0137
www.geodeck.com

HandyDeck Systems
2201 Distribution Circle
Silver Spring, MD 20910
Tel: 866 206 8316
www.deckingtiles.com

Hickory Dickory Decks
115 Dundas Street / HWY 5
Flamborough, ON, Canada
Tel: 800 263 4774
www.hickorydickorydecks.com

Louisiana-Pacific Corporation
P.O. Box 7429
Endicott, NY 13761
Tel: 888 820 0325
www.lpcorp.com

Maine Deck
Maine House
54 Meadow Way
Verwood, Dorset
BH31 6HG, England
Tel: +44 7803 957712
www.maine-deck.co.uk

Rhino Deck
One Master Mark Drive
P.O. Box 662
Albany, MN 56307-0662
Tel: 800 535 4838
www.rhinodeck.com

Tamko Building Products
P.O. Box 1404
Joplin, MO 64802
Tel: 800 253 1401
www.evergrain.com

Thermal Industries
5450 Second Avenue
Pittsburg, PA 15207
Tel: 800 245 1540
www.thermalindustries.com

Tiger Claw
400 Middle Street
Suite J
Bristol, CT 06010-8405
Tel: 800 928 4437
www.deckfastener.com

TimberTech Limited
894 Prairie Avenue
Wilmington, OH 45177
Tel: 800 307 7780
www.timbertech.com

Trex
160 Exeter Drive
Winchester, VA 22603
Tel: 800 289 8739
www.trex.com

Wolmanized Wood
1955 Lake Park Drive
Suite 100
Smyrna, GA 30080
Tel: 770 801 6600
www.wolmanizedwood.com

PATIOS & MATERIALS

Daltile
7834 C.F. Hawn Fwy
Dallas, TX 75217
Tel: 214 398 1411
www.daltileproducts.com

Earth'n Wood Landscape Supply
5335 Strausser Street NW
North Canton, OH 44720
Tel: 330 499 8309
www.earthnwood.com

Oldcastle Architectural Products
375 Northridge Road
Suite 250
Atlanta, GA 30350
Tel: 800 899 8455
www.belgard.biz

Rock Unique
Main Road, Sundridge
Kent, TN14 6ED
England
Tel: +44 1959 565 608
www.rock-unique.com

SAE Builders
2052 Daffodil Way
Hemet, CA 92545
Tel: 951 658 5807 or 760 776 9660
www.saebuilders.com

Telluride Stone Company
P.O. Box 3552
Telluride, CO 81435
Tel: 970 728 6201
www.telluridestone.com

Wausau Tile
P.O. Box 1520
Wausau, WI 54402
Tel: 800 388 8728
www.wausautile.com

PAINTS & STAINS

Behr
3400 West Segerstrom Avenue
Santa Ana, CA 92704
Tel: 714 545 7101
www.behr.com

The Flood Company
P.O. Box 2535
Hudson, OH 44236
Tel: 800 321 3444
www.flood.com

Olympic
PPG Industries
1 PPG Place
Pittsburg, PA 15272
Tel: 800 441 9695
www.olympic.com

Pratt & Lambert
P.O. Box 22
Buffalo, NY 14240
Tel: 800 289 7728
www.prattandlambert.com

Sherwin-Williams Company
101 Prospect Avenue, NW
Cleveland, OH 44115
Tel: 800 474 37946
www.sherwin-williams.com

ACCESSORIES

Awnings.US
awnings
15 Dixon Street
Shelbyville, DE 19975
Tel: 800 838 8821
www.awnings.us

Cadix
furniture, outdoor lighting, planters
Unit 6, Two Counties Estate,
Falconer Road, Haverhill
Suffolk, CB9 7XZ
England
Tel: +44 1440 713 704
www.cadix.co.uk

The Cedar Station
furniture
8175 Wichita Hill Drive
Indianapolis, IN 46217
Tel: 877 270 8185
www.thecedarstation.com

CedarStore.com
furniture
5410 Route 8
Gibsonia, PA 15044
Tel: 888 293 2339
www.cedarstore.com

Decks USA
deck accessory plans
97 Karago Avenue
Suite 5
Boardman, OH 44512
Tel: 330 726 5540
www.decksusa.com

Deck Way
furniture, arbors, pergolas
P.O. Box 4296
Montgomery, AL 36103
Tel: 877 332 5929
www.deckway.com

Everywhere Chair LLC
furniture
24 North Main Street
Burnsville, NC 28714
Tel: 828 678 9660
www.everywherechair.com

Fire Stone
grills
12400 Portland Ave. South
Suite 195
Burnsville, MN 55337
Tel: 866 303 4028
www.firestonehp.com

Garden Winds
general patio and deck accessories
4950 East Second Street
Benicia, CA 94510
Tel: 877 479 4637
www.gardenwinds.com

Hampton Bay
furniture
The Home Depot
1971 West Lumsden Road
Brandon, FL 33511
Tel: 877 430 3376
www.hamptonbay.com

Home Infatuation
fans, storage boxes, heaters, wood patio tiles, outdoor furniture covers
250 East Main Street
Suite 209
Galesburg, IL 61401
Tel: 877 224 8925
www.homeinfatuation.com

LA Patio
furniture, swings
4225 Prado Road
Suite 108
Corona, CA 92880
Tel: 888 937 2846
www.lapatio.com

Lighting For Gardens
outdoor lighting
20 Furmston Court
Icknield Way
Letchworth Garden City
Herts, SG6 1UJ
England
Tel: +44 1462 486 777
www.lightingforgardens.com

Malibu Intermatic
outdoor lighting
Intermatic Plaza
Spring Grove, IL 60081
Tel: 815 675 7000
www.intermatic.com

Olympic Hot Tub
hot tubs
1425 Dexter Ave. North
Seattle, WA 98109
Tel: 800 448 8814 / 206 286 0700
www.olympichottub.com

OutbackPatio.com
furniture
138 West 2260 South
Salt Lake City, UT 84115
Tel: 801 486 4156
www.outbackpatio.com

Outdoor Kitchens by First Place
outdoor kitchens
5523 SE International Way
Portland, OR 97222
Tel: 503 659 5666
www.outdoorkitchens.com

Patio and Garden
outdoor lights, benches, planters, fountains
1045 Hensley Street
Richmond, CA 94801
Tel: 800 761 5222
www.patio-and-garden.com

PatioUmbrellas.com
patio umbrellas
12720 I Street
Suite 200
Omaha, NE 68137
Tel: 800 625 6614
www.patioumbrellas.com

Poly-Wood
furniture
1001 West Brooklyn Street
Syracuse, IN 46567
Tel: 574 457 3284 / 877 457 3284
www.polywoodinc.com

Rausch Classics
furniture
An der Tagweide 14
76139 Karlsruhe
Germany
Tel: +49 721 96169-0
www.rausch-classics.de

Retractable Awnings
awnings
16255 NW 54th Ave.
Miami Gardens, FL 33014-6106
Tel: 866 438 2964
www.retractableawnings.com

Shade Sails
shade structures
7028 Greenleaf Ave.
Suite K
Whittier, CA 90602
Tel: 562 945 9952
www.shadesails.com

ShadeTree Canopies
6317 Busch Blvd
Columbus, OH 43229
Tel: 614 844 5990
www.shadetreecanopies.com

Smith & Hawken
furniture
P.O. Box 8690
Pueblo, CO 81008
Tel: 800 940 1170
www.smithandhawken.com

SunSetter Products
shade structures
184 Charles Street
Malden, MA 02148
Tel: 800 876 2340
www.sunsetter.com

Today's Pool & Patio
furniture
23616 North 19th Avenue
Phoenix, AZ 85027
Tel: 800 457 0305
www.todayspatio.com

Tropitone
furniture
1401 Commerce Blvd
Sarasota, FL 34243
Tel: 941 355 2715
www.tropitone.com

Weber-Stephen Products
grills
200 East Daniels Road
Palatine, IL 60067
Tel: 800 446 1071
www.weber.com

Wer/Ever Products
outdoor kitchens
3900 South 50th Street
Tampa, FL 33619
Tel: 888 324 3837
www.werever.com

Index

Acknowledgments

The publishers would like to thank the following companies for their invaluable assistance: Artisan Quality Decks, Association of Pool and Spa Professionals (APSP), Cadix, CertainTeed, Decking For Less, DecKorators, Divine Construction, Elyria Fence, Fire Stone, The Flood Company, Fortress Iron, Hampton Bay, HandyDeck Systems, Hickory Dickory Decks, Lighting For Gardens, Maine Deck, Patio Enclosures, Inc., Poly-Wood, Rausch Classics, Retractable Awnings, Rhino Deck, SAE Builders, Shade Sails, Southern Pine Council, Tiger Claw, Trex, Tropitone, Wolmanized Wood.

Front cover: Lighting For Gardens
Back cover: Cadix
2 © Tim Street-Porter/Beateworks/Corbis
4–5 © John Edward Linden/Arcaid/Corbis
6 Corbis © Tim Street-Porter/Beateworks/Corbis
7 Corbis © Alan Weintraub/Arcaid/Corbis
8–9 1, 2 Hickory Dickory Decks/Drew Cunningham, Canada; 3 Association of Pool and Spa Professionals (APSP)
10–11 1 Trex; 2 CertainTeed; 3 APSP; 4 The Flood Company
16–17 1 Rock Unique; 2 APSP; 3 HandyDeck Systems; 4 The Flood Company
18–19 1 Rausch Classics; 2 © Tim Street-Porter/Beateworks/Corbis; 3 SAE Builders, 4 Andreas von Einsiedel/Designer: Mary Gilliatt; 5 CertainTeed
20–21 1 Ken Hayden/Redcover.com Architect & Designer: Terry Hunziker; 2 Lighting For Gardens; 3 Cadix; 4 Wolmanized Wood;
22 Wolmanized Wood
23 Fortress Iron
24–25 1–6 Hickory Dickory Decks/Drew Cunningham, Canada
26–27 1–7 Hickory Dickory Decks/Drew Cunningham, Canada
28–29 1, 2 Trex; 3–6 Hickory Dickory Decks/Drew Cunningham, Canada
30–31 1–7 Hickory Dickory Decks/Drew Cunningham, Canada
32–33 1 Hickory Dickory Decks/Drew Cunningham, Canada; 2 Patio Enclosures, Inc; 3 Hickory Dickory Decks/Drew Cunningham, Canada; 4 Divine Construction; 5 Fortress Iron
34–35 1 Tiger Claw; 2–4 Hickory Dickory Decks/Drew Cunningham, Canada
36–37 1, 3 The Flood Company; 2, 4 Trex
38–39 1 The Flood Company; 2, 3, 5 Hickory Dickory Decks/Drew Cunningham, Canada; 4, 6 Divine Construction
40–41 1 The Flood Company; 2 Decking For Less; 3 Hickory Dickory Decks/Drew Cunningham, Canada; 4 Southern Pine Council; 6 Fortress Iron; 7 Elyria Fence
42–43 1 Trex; 2–4 Hickory Dickory Decks/Drew Cunningham, Canada; 5 The Flood Company; 6 © Brenda A. Smith/Fotolia.com; 7 Fortress Iron

44–45 1–5 Hickory Dickory Decks/Drew Cunningham, Canada
46–47 1 Divine Construction; 2 Wolmanized Wood; 3–5 Hickory Dickory Decks/Drew Cunningham, Canada
50–51 1 Shade Sails; 2 CertainTeed; 3, 4 DecKorators; 5, 6, 8 Decking For Less; 7 Tiger Claw; 9 Wolmanized Wood
54–55 1 Divine Construction; 2 Hickory Dickory Decks/Drew Cunningham, Canada; 3 © Tim Street-Porter/Beateworks/Corbis; 4, 5 Fortress Iron; 6 Southern Pine Council
56–57 1, 5 Fortress Iron; 2 Divine Construction; 3 Wolmanized Wood; 4 Southern Pine Council
58–59 1 Divine Construction; 5–7 Hickory Dickory Decks/Drew Cunningham, Canada
60 Bieke Claessens/Redcover.com
61 Ken Hayden/Redcover.com Architect & Designer: Terry Hunziker
68–69 1 N Minh & J Wass/Redcover.com; 2 Grey Crawford/Redcover.com; 3, 5, 7 Rausch Classics; 4 Hampton Bay; 6 Grey Crawford/Redcover.com Architect: Steven Ehrlich
70–71 1, 2 Hickory Dickory Decks/Drew Cunningham, Canada; 3 Craig Fraser/Redcover.com Architect: Fabian, Hackner & Berman; 4 Fortress Iron; 5 SAE Builders; 6 Rausch Classics
72–73 1 Andreas von Einsiedel/Designer: Virginia Bates; 2 Karyn Millet/Redcover.com Designer: Patricia Benner; 3 Sunniva Harte/Redcover.com; 4 Rausch Classics; 5 © Tine Eelman/Fotolia.com; 6 Tropitone; 7 APSP
76–77 1 © Ernesto Lopez/Fotolia.com; 2 © Marti Timple/Fotolia.com; 3 Hickory Dickory Decks/Drew Cunningham, Canada; 4 © Rob Marmion/Fotolia.com; 5 APSP; 6 Henry Wilson/Redcover.com Designer: Voon Yee Wong; 7 © Tiffany Jones/Fotolia.com
78 1 Hickory Dickory Decks/Drew Cunningham, Canada
80–81 1, 3–5 APSP; 2 Neil Corder/Redcover.com Architect: Van Der Merwe Miszewski Architects
82–83 1 © Ariel Bravy/Fotolia.com; 2 Andreas von Einsiedel/Designer: John

Stefanidis; 3 © Larry Roberg/Fotolia.com; 4 Andreas von Einsiedel/Designer: Julie Gibson Jarvie; 5 © Kevin Miller/Fotolia.com
84–85 1 Andreas von Einsiedel/Designer: Alex Dingwall-Main; 2 © asist/Fotolia.com; 3 Christopher Drake/Redcover.com Architect: Philip Wagner Designer: Binny Hudson; 4 Andreas von Einsiedel/Designer: Candy & Candy; 5 Grey Crawford/Redcover.com; 6 Andreas von Einsiedel/Designer: John Leaning
86–87 1, 6 APSP; 2 © Chris Hill/Fotolia.com; 3 Andreas von Einsiedel/Designer: Todhunter Earle; 4 Hickory Dickory Decks/Drew Cunningham, Canada; 5 Andreas von Einsiedel/Designer: Bonnie Morris
90–91 1 Andreas von Einsiedel/Designer: Niels Hansen and Steffen Reimers; 2 Lighting For Gardens; 3 Andreas von Einsiedel/Designer: Legorreta & Legorreta Architects; 4 Andreas von Einsiedel/Designer: Philippa Naess; 5 Andreas von Einsiedel/Designer: Holger Stewen; 6 Andreas von Einsiedel/Designer: John Stefanidis; 7 Bieke Claessens/Redcover.com
92–93 1 © ondacaracola/Fotolia.com; 2 © Giuseppe Porzani/Fotolia.com; 3 © marilyna/Fotolia.com; 4 © Peter Hogstrom/Fotolia.com; 5 © Jean-louis Bouzou/Fotolia.com; 6, 10 © imagepro/Fotolia.com; 7 © Kirsty Pargeter/Fotolia.com; 8 © Beatrice Zagano/Fotolia.com; 9 © Scrivener/Fotolia.com; 11 © Hugo Real/Fotolia.com; 12 © Timothy Norcia/Fotolia.com
94–95 1 APSP; 2 Andreas von Einsiedel/Designer: Malcom Hillier; 3 Andreas von Einsiedel/Designer: Monique Waque; 4 Andreas von Einsiedel/Designer: Holger Stewen; 5, 6 SAE Builders
96–97 1 Andreas von Einsiedel/Designer: Legorreta & Legorreta Architects; 2 Andreas von Einsiedel/Architecture & Restoration: Bruno et Alexandre Lafourcade, 10 Boulevard Victor Hugo 13210 St Remy de Provence. France Tel. +33 490 921014; 3 © Michael Boys/Corbis; 4 Hickory Dickory Decks/Drew Cunningham, Canada; 5 SAE Builders
98–99 1–5 Hickory Dickory Decks/Drew

Cunningham, Canada
100 The Flood Company
101 Divine Construction
102–103 1, 6, 7 Fortress Iron; 2 CertainTeed; 3 Wolmanized Wood; 4, 5 Divine Construction
104–105 1, 3, 5, 6 Hickory Dickory Decks/ Drew Cunningham, Canada; 2 Divine Construction; 4 Fortress Iron
106–107 1, 2, 4, 6 Fortress Iron; 3, 5 Hickory Dickory Decks/Drew Cunningham, Canada
108–109 1 Fortress Iron; 2–5 Hickory Dickory Decks/Drew Cunningham, Canada
110–111 1, 3–5 Hickory Dickory Decks/ Drew Cunningham, Canada; 2, 6 Fortress Iron
112–113 1 Decking For Less; 2, 4–6 Hickory Dickory Decks/Drew Cunningham, Canada; 3 Divine Construction
130–131 1 The Flood Company; 2, 4, 5 Divine Construction; 3 Hickory Dickory Decks/Drew Cunningham, Canada
132 Bieke Claessens/Redcover.com
133 © Elenathewise/Fotolia.com
134–135 1 Andreas von Einsiedel/Designer: Reinhard Weiss, 3S Architects; 2, 5 Hampton Bay; 3 Retractable Awnings; 4 Grey Ryan & Sally Beyer/Redcover.com; 6 APSP
138–139 1 © Adrian Hillman/Fotolia.com; 2 Fire Stone; 3, 5, 7 APSP; 4 Rausch Classics; 6 Tropitone
140–141 1, 2, 5, 6, 9, 13, 17 Daltile; 3, 4, 7, 8 Mandarin Stone; 10, 11, 14, 15, 18, 19 Bettini Tile Service; 12, 16, 20 Indigenous
142–143 1, 3 Rausch Classics; 2 Hampton Bay; 4 Dan Duchars/Redcover.com
144–145 1 Daltile; 2 Fortress Iron; 3 Tropitone; 4 Elyria Fence; 5 Poly-Wood; 6 Rausch Classics
146–147 1–4 Daltile, 5–7 © Timothy Norcia/ Fotolia.com; 8 © Marti Timple/Fotolia.com; 9, 11 © Luke Heffernan/Fotolia.com; 10 © Chris Harvey/Fotolia.com; 12 © almagami/ Fotolia.com
148–149 1, 4, 6 Retractable Awnings; 2 APSP; 3, 5 Rausch Classics; 7 Hickory Dickory Decks/Drew Cunningham, Canada
150–153 Daltile
154–155 1, 5 Hickory Dickory Decks/Drew Cunningham, Canada; 2, 3 Fire Stone; 4 APSP; 6 Divine Construction
156–157 1 © Mike Thompson/Fotolia.com; 2–7 © Timothy Norcia/Fotolia.com; 8, 11 © James Cox/Fotolia.com; 9 © Andrew Dierks/Fotolia.com; 10 © Kurt Holter/ Fotolia.com; 12 © Nadejda Degtyareva/ Fotolia.com
158–159 1 Dan Duchars/Redcover.com; 2 Andreas von Einsiedel/Designer: Holger Stewen; 3 Simon McBride/Redcover.com; 4 APSP; 5 Andreas von Einsiedel/Designer:

Joe and Mary Hope; 6 Graham Atkins-Hughes/Redcover.com
160–161 1 © Olga D. Van De Veer/Fotolia. com; 2 © Andy Spliethof/Fotolia.com; 3 © Vadim Kozlovsky/Fotolia.com; 4 © Irina Belousa/Fotolia.com; 5, 6 © Baloncici/ Fotolia.com; 7 © Kasia75/Fotolia.com; 8 © jlye/Fotolia.com; 9 © Jerome Bertin/ Fotolia.com; 10 © imagepro/Fotolia.com; 11 © Scott Ramon/Fotolia.com; 12 © Elenathewise/Fotolia.com
162–163 1, 3, 4 HandyDeck Systems; 2 Grant Govier/Redcover.com; 5 Ed Reeve/ Redcover.com; 6 Andreas von Einsiedel/ Designer: Candy & Candy; 7 Ken Hayden/ Redcover.com Designer: Nigel Pearce
164–165 1 Southern Pine Council; 2 Simon McBride/Redcover.com Designer: Anna Raven; 3 Grant Govier/Redcover. com; 4 Johnny Bouchier/Redcover.com; 5 Tropitone; 6 Rausch Classics; 7 Grey Crawford/Redcover.com Designer: Katerina Tana
166 Tropitone
167 Hampton Bay
168–169 1, 2, 4 Fire Stone; 3 Hampton Bay; 5 © Najlah Feanny/Corbis; 6 © Jyothi Joshi/Fotolia.com
170–171 1 Wolmanized Wood; 2, 7 Fire Stone; 3 Chloe Johnson/Alamy; 4 Andreas von Einsiedel/Designer: Pedro de Azambuja; 5 Hickory Dickory Decks/ Drew Cunningham, Canada; 6 Konrad Zelazowski/Alamy
172–173 1 Fire Stone; 2–4 Rausch Classics; 5 Wolmanized Wood; 6 Hampton Bay; 7 Patio Enclosures, Inc; 8 Tropitone
174–175 1, 4, 5 Hampton Bay; 2, 6 Poly-Wood; 3, 7, 8 Tropitone
176–177 1 James Mitchell/Redcover.com; 2 Cadix; 3 Trex; 4 Hampton Bay; 5 The Flood Company; 6 Rausch Classics; 7 Patio Enclosures, Inc
178–179 1 Andreas von Einsiedel/Designer: Candy & Candy; 2, 3, 5 Hickory Dickory Decks/Drew Cunningham, Canada; 4 Amanda Turner/Redcover.com; 6 © Andrea Rugg Photography/Beateworks/Corbis
180–181 1 © Zlatko Antunic/Fotolia.com; 2–5, 7, 9–11 Cadix; 6 © Manfred Ament/ Fotolia.com; 8 © Loredana/Fotolia.com
182–183 Cadix
184–185 1–8, 10 Cadix; 9 © Tomasz Adamczyk/Fotolia.com
186–187 APSP
188–189 1–4, 6 APSP; 5 Andreas von Einsiedel/Architecture: Michael Drain. Decoration: Sarah Vanrenen
190–191 1, 5 Hickory Dickory Decks/Drew Cunningham, Canada; 2 Andreas von Einsiedel/Designer: Lady Annabel Astor; 3 Andreas von Einsiedel/Architects: Guard,

Tillman, Pollock Ltd; 4, 6 APSP
192–193 1, 5 APSP; 2 Maine Deck; 3 Tropitone; 4 Rhino Deck; 6 Andreas von Einsiedel/Designer: Pedro de Azambuja
194–195 1, 6 Cadix; 2 Anthony Harrison/ Redcover.com; 3 Tropitone; 4 Dan Duchars/Redcover.com; 5 APSP; 7 Rausch Classics
196–199 Cadix
200–201 1 Andreas von Einsiedel/Designer: Gordon Gardiner; 2 Divine Construction; 3 Wolmanized Wood; 4 Hickory Dickory Decks/Drew Cunningham, Canada; 5 DecKorators; 6 © Elenathewise/Fotolia.com
202–203 1 Retractable Awnings; 2 Ken Hayden/Redcover.com Architect: John Pawson; 3 Southern Pine Council; 4 SAE Builders; 5 Tropitone; 6, 7 APSP
204–205 1 Southern Pine Council; 2, 3, 5 Hickory Dickory Decks/Drew Cunningham, Canada; 4 Tropitone; 6 APSP; 7 The Flood Company
206–207 1 Trex; 2, 3 Hickory Dickory Decks/ Drew Cunningham, Canada; 4 Tropitone
208–209 1 Tropitone; 2 Rausch Classics; 3 Artisan Quality Decks; 4 Fire Stone; 5 Wolmanized Wood; 6, 7 SAE Builders
210–211 1 Fortress Iron; 2–4, 6 Hickory Dickory Decks/Drew Cunningham, Canada; 5 DecKorators
212–213 1, 5 APSP; 2, 3 Hickory Dickory Decks/Drew Cunningham, Canada; 4 Decking For Less; 6 Patio Enclosures, Inc
214–215 1 Hampton Bay; 2, 5 Tropitone; 3, 9 Shade Sails; 4 Maine Deck; 6, 7 Patio Enclosures, Inc; 8 Retractable Awnings
216–217 1 James Balston/Redcover.com Architect: Bloc; 2 Hickory Dickory Decks/Drew Cunningham, Canada; 3 © dbvirago/Fotolia.com; 4 Shade Sails; 5 Cadix
218–219 1, 3 Fire Stone; 2 Trex; 4 Hampton Bay; 5, 7 APSP; 6 Tropitone
220–221 1 Artisan Quality Decks; 2–4, 6, 7 APSP; 5 Fire Stone
222–223 1 Cadix; 2, 4 Hampton Bay; 3 Fire Stone
224–225 Cadix
226–227 1, 3–5 Divine Construction; 2 Fortress Iron